W9-BHE-736

# FISHING SOLUTIONS

## MEMBER TIPS & TACTICS

North American Fishing Club
Minnetonka, MN

# FISHING SOLUTIONS

## MEMBER TIPS & TACTICS

# ACKNOWLEDGEMENTS

**We would like to thank NAFC members for sending their favorite fishing tips as the foundation for *Fishing Solutions—Member Tips & Tactics*.**

Mike Vail
*Vice President, Product and Business Development*

Tom Carpenter
*Director of Book and New Media Development*

Dan Kennedy
*Book Production Manager*

Michele Teigen
*Book Development Coordinator*

Todd Sauers
*Book Design and Production*

Dan Kennedy
Brook Martin
Bill Lindner Photography
*Photography*

Kenny Kaiser
Joe Tomelleri
*Illustration*

Kelly Gohman
*Fishing Tip Editor*

Copyright ©1999 North American Fishing Club

All rights reserved. No part of this publication may be reproduced, stored in an electronic retrieval system or transmitted in any form or by any means (electronic, mechanical, photocopying, recording or otherwise) without the prior written permission of the copyright owner.

10 9 8 7 6 5 4 3 2 1

ISBN 1-58159-064-4

North American Fishing Club
12301 Whitewater Drive
Minnetonka, MN 55343

# TABLE OF CONTENTS

# INTRODUCTION

Luck has a place in fishing, that's for sure. But it's also true that anglers make a lot of their own luck. How? For starters, just being there—out on the water, fishing hard—is the first and most critical step to success. You won't catch any fish while sitting on your couch thinking about it.

So just being there is important; but so are the details, for fishing most surely is a game of "little things" that, when strung together just so, bring fish to your waiting hand or net. That's what *Fishing Solutions—Member Tips & Tactics* is all about.

Here are hundreds of years of fishing experience—directly from the great fish-catching members of the North American Fishing Club—rolled into one photo-, illustration- and idea-packed book. You'll read about casting, lures, baits, tackle storage ideas, boats, rods & reels … and of course there are dozens upon dozens of tactics and tips for finding and catching fish of all kinds.

This book has one simple purpose: to pass on to you plenty of tips, tactics, ideas and advice that will help you bring all the details of fishing together even better, to help you catch more fish, more often, every time you hit the water.

Good luck, good fishing!

## Chapter One

# 1 CASTING

**I**t seems pretty basic, how to cast. But at second glance, there's a lot more to it than meets the eye: getting good distance; dropping your lure, bait or fly right where it's supposed to be; and preventing backlashes and other assorted snarls. NAFC members have some good ideas for improving their casting skills and efficiency, and here's what they have to say.

# Bottom Fishing

When bottom fishing for striped bass or catfish, I will make my cast and let it settle to the bottom. Then I will pull a little slack in my line in front of the reel and clip a small bobber on the line. When I get a strike or a pickup, the bobber is a sure giveaway.

*John Hempsmyer*
*Redwood Valley, CA*

# No More Tangles

I fish in a small pond where my line frequently gets caught on logs and tree limbs under water. Instead of cutting the line whenever it breaks, I pull my line back, almost to the point of breaking, and then let the line out very fast. Most of the time this works great.

*Jordan Cunningham*
*Durham, NC*

# Increased Casting Distance

I discovered a great way to get more casting distance out of my fly line. I use a mild, vinyl seat protectant such as Armor All to clean the line. Not only does it clean the line, the protectant gives it a slick finish, which I believe allows the line to flow more freely through the line guides. Simply hold a shop rag in one hand and spray it well with the protectant. Close your fist, pull the fly line through and you're in business.

*Brian Hilbert*
*Powell, WY*

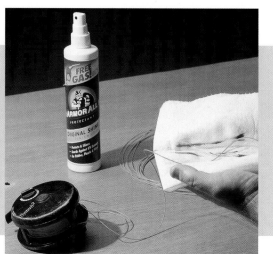

# Casting Remedy

Whenever you cast a bait over a limb, there's a trick to getting it free. When the lure swings back and forth, don't wait until it moves away from you, because it puts the bait in line with the branch and it usually gets caught when you apply pressure. The 'secret' lies in waiting until the lure swings towards you then pull the rod so the lure is thrown back and over the limb.

*Steve VonBrandt*
*Wilmington, DE*

# Baitcaster Backlashes

To prevent serious backlashes follow these directions. Make a long cast with your baitcaster, pull out your line another yard and take a piece of electrical tape and wrap it around the spool. This will prevent the spool from overrunning past the tape.

*William Warren*
*Roxboro, NC*

# Casting for Distance

To maintain the smooth, long distance cast we all desire, it's important to tune-up even our new spinning reels at least twice a year. First clear the line off the spool. Then, using a buffing wheel on a drill, buff the edge of the spool until smooth. I use either an aluminum or plastic buffing compound. I can feel the difference by touch as well as the improved performance.

*David Wiggs*
*Carterville, IL*

# Not Your Average Cast

When I was out fly fishing during the summer, I saw a group of good-size bass in a slow current spot on the river. I wanted to find a new approach to getting them to strike. I reached over and grabbed a leaf and set my fly on it. I gave myself a lot of slack so my fly would drift right to the spot I wanted. When my fly got close enough for the bass to see it, I started shaking my line until the fly fell off. I think the fly falling off the leaf resembled an ant falling off a piece of bark or leaf. This method proved very worthy. I caught 3 out of the 5 bass.

*Doug Wesserling*
*Dearborn Heights, MI*

# Casting Methods with Wet Flies

Since wet flies simulate dead insects, or live ones barely moving, they are usually drifted in currents or fished slowly in currentless water. Casts are planned to direct the flies through holding positions or feeding lanes, at the level of the fish, which normally is close to bottom.

One favorite method of fishing wet flies in streams is the "dead drift," as used with streamers, except that little, if any action is given to the flies. The current does the work. Cast upstream and across to let the flies run deep and mend the line, upstream or downstream as necessary, to keep the cast at current speed. Small subcurrents work on one fly, which activates the others in natural-appearing movement.

An exciting dividend when using more than one fly on a leader is that when they drift into a potential position, a trout may grab one of them. Not to be outdone, another fish or two may strike the others. Conservation-minded anglers may question the ethics of multiple-fly use, but hopefully users will have "catch-and-release" in mind.

To fish the best wet fly patterns for local waters, check with a local tackle shop.

# Side Arm Solutions

Side arm is the best way to cast if the wind is blowing strongly off the water because with the side cast, you'll be whipping your casting weight on a horizontal plane.

*Leo Seffelaar*
*Broadview, Saskatchewan, Canada*

# Down Home Weed Eater

Fishing vegetation is fun and productive, but can be a pain in the neck. Hang ups commonly occur, usually resulting in lost lures. To remedy this problem I use a fillet knife taped to an extendable crappie pole. This will work on most any type of vegetation, including lilypads and hydrilla.

*Coleby Gilliand*
*Deatsville, AL*

# Smoother Fly Fishing Casts

**W**hen fly fishing for steelhead, anglers typ-ically use split-shot to help get the fly down deep. I've found that the lead twist-on weights, which resemble matchsticks, are much better. Not only do they help create a smoother cast, but the streamlined weight creates a more natural swing when streamer fishing. Plus, you can use as little, or as much as you like.

*Jonathan Storm*
*Senior Editor, North American Fisherman*

# Underhand Casts

**T**he underhand or flip cast is the approved method when you're on a high perch over the water fishing pier, bridge or bulk-head when there are low over-hangs or tree branches that might entangle your line. Here's how to do it: Point the rod tip straight out in front of you. Flip it down, whip it up again and let go of your line. Your lure won't cast as far as the sidearm or overhead cast, but it usually will fetch the opposite river or canal bank, perhaps providing more accu-racy too.

*Leo Seffelaar*
*Broadview, Saskatchewan,*
*Canada*

# Practice. Practice. Practice.

**E**ver wonder how those guys on TV make all those perfect casts between trees and whatever other obstacles are in the way? It's a little thing called practice. These people fish all the time...that's how they make their living. If you're like me, you can't fish everyday. If you don't go through the repetitions of practice, then you can't get better. So what do you do if you're unable to go to the lake everyday? I set up a casting course in my backyard. I started with large targets like old tires. I placed them at different places throughout the yard. I made sure some were difficult to hit (like next to trees and bushes). I put a sinker on my line and practiced casting to those spots. I practiced casting overhand, underhand and side armed. You never know when you'll be in a situation that dictates how you have to cast. So it's a good policy to get as proficient at all the different ways as you can, just in case. After you've mastered hitting the bigger targets, place smaller targets in the same places and practice hitting those. Your accuracy will increase and you'll be able to get your cast to go into those little hard to get places where it seems the fish always are. And when you're out fishing and you're able to get into the spots you want to, you'll enjoy fishing even more. So get out there and practice!

*Dennis Temby*
*Midland, TX*

# Casting in Tight Spots

Bow and arrow is the best way to cast when fishing in truly tight spots such as web-like brush that often surrounds a particularly good freshwater hole or weed patch. Here's how to do it: Release enough line for your casting weight to hang midway down your rod, grab it and pull it firmly toward you. Your rod will bend like a bow under the pressure. Point it at your target, which is now at nine o'clock, let go the weight and an instant later open your trigger finger. That's all there is to it. No arm motion, no wrist snap, but your terminal rigging will propel it across the water like an arrow.

*Leo Seffelaar*
*Broadview, Saskatchewan, Canada*

# Retrieving Bad Casts

When you're casting spinnerbaits or other lures to bass in flooded timber, whether shoreline or standing trees in reservoirs, you'll inevitably hang a bait over a tree or brush limb. To avoid wasting precious fishing time by retrieving it with your boat, pull it free with the pendulum approach. As the lure swings back and forth suspended below the limb, give it a sharp jerk when it swings toward you. This will cause the bait to swing upward in an arc and clear the limb on its way back to the boat. If you pull when the bait is swinging away from you, it will be pulled right into the branch and you'll need to move in with the boat to free it. Baits that wrap around a limb two or three times are much harder to free. To avoid this problem, when you see a cast is "going long" and you're going to drop a bait over a limb, don't panic. Give the lure slack line to drop straight down after it clears the limb. That way, it won't swing around and wrap the line around the branch. Then, it's only a quick pendulum swing from freedom.

*Dan Johnson*
*Senior Editor, North American Fisherman*

# Time to Cast

There is a casting method I use that is very effective. First of all, picture you and your rod as a clock viewed from above. You are the center and the rod is the hour hand. If you are right-handed, hold the rod in your right hand with elbow bent at 3 o'clock. If you are left-handed, hold the rod in your left hand with elbow bent at 9 o'clock. Then, for either left-handed people or right-handed people, in one movement press the release button or release the line as you snap your wrist forward to 12 o'clock. If you did it right, your cast should land near your target. After a few practices, you should be able to land your cast almost on the target. I must warn you however when you use my method, most fish when hit by a lure doing 60 mph, will swim off in a blind panic.

*Tracy Benton*
*Boca Raton, FL*

# 2

# LURES

There seems to be no end to the different ways you can rig or fish artificial lures, or to the ways you can customize them to meet specific fishing needs. After all, if fishermen and women were afraid to experiment, we probably wouldn't catch many fish at all. NAFC members were generous enough to share the results of their explorations here, in hopes that maybe you can hit the right pattern or combination sooner, next time you're out on the water.

# Extended Lure Life

Here's an idea that saved me money and helped me catch more fish. Sooner or later we all pass down lures to our kids and sometimes even our fishing partners. Well, our kids we can borrow back, but put a hold on those passes to your buddy. Especially if the spinners are those old flatfish like grand-dad used to use. By adding a bucktail to those old spinners and maybe changing the blades (or simply polishing), for a lot less than a new purchase you can have new fish-catching appeal. Those flatfish are another story. If the color is still good, consider a coating of clear sparkling nail polish; the newer kinds with sparkle flakes work wonders in adding that little extra. One more trick I do with my flatfish is to remove the front treble and add a bucktail to the rear. Often the old standby colors of red and white (with maribou feathers for extra body) can be the difference between a fish and no fish. The jointed action of the bucktail will bring more strikes than conventional flatfish almost two to one in pressured waters. And because of the body of the tail, I've found you can fish it slower and shallower with better results. These suggestions work great for northern pike and largemouth bass. The missing hook on the flatfish hasn't harmed hooking percentages and reduces foul-ups.

*R. Ballard*
*Benzonia, MI*

# Modified Buzzbait

When fishing a buzzbait, drill 3 or 4 holes in the bent portion of the blade. File down the bars by the holes which make the lure bubble and attract big bass from deep water and thick cover.

*Tim Cronin*
*Phoenix, AZ*

# Cold-Weather Fishing

When fishing in extremely cold temperatures, trim your line close to your knot. That prevents icing up so not to affect the wobble of your lures.

*Justin Albert*
*Liverpool, PA*

# Fishing After a Cold Front

After a cold front, a lot of fishermen think that bass are completely uncatchable, but for those that have patience, the result will be rewarding. A good method of presentation is to take a 4- to 6-inch grape colored worm and pitch it in next to boulders and weeds. Let it lie there for several minutes without moving it. This presentation, called 'dead worm' by some anglers, proves itself a winner over and over.

*Jeremy Gooch*
*Sturgis, MI*

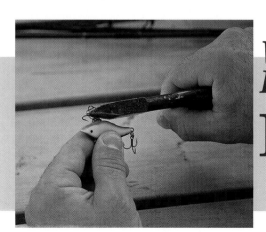

# Weedless Crankbait Fishing

If you are fishing a weedy area with a crankbait, take the crankbait and clip off the treble hook's prongs that face the front of the lure. This makes the crankbait virtually weedless.

*Jeremy Gooch*
*Sturgis, MI*

# Midwinter

It usually takes a month or so for the onset of what we call the midwinter period. Mostly, it has to do with oxygen levels. Heavy snow cover early—which cuts off light penetration and photosynthesis sooner—will accelerate the process, whereas years of less snow will slow it down.

At "early" midwinter, the first reaction of fish, generally speaking, is to spend more time in deeper water. The water is warmest, generally 39 degrees Fahrenheit, at the bottom of a frozen lake (and slightly above 32 just under the ice). As long as adequate oxygen holds out at the bottom of deep-water areas, they will hold lots of fish. But eventually, oxygen levels at the bottom can deteriorate also. (Bottom "ooze" eats oxygen.) It's common at this time of year to see fish begin to suspend more. In lakes with a lot of vegetation and mucky sediment, late-midwinter fish can be sort of "forced into the middle zone" of the water column. It could be a combination of environmental factors, that together leave the middle of the water column the best compromise zone of temperature and oxygen.

Some experts also believe this fish suspension could be a plankton-driven phenomenon. Masses of plankton might, for example, "layer out" at certain levels of light intensity. That would draw baitfish and panfish, and in turn larger predators. You'll see concentrations of plankton on a good depthfinder, and will notice that they move up and down in response to changing light conditions.

Again, keep in mind that the timing and severity of the "oxygen problem" is regulated by the makeup of the body of water and the amount of snow cover. Generally speaking, deeper, less fertile lakes hold oxygen better than shallower, more fertile lakes; larger lakes hold oxygen better than smaller ones. A small, deep lake is not as likely to suffer "freeze-out" (where oxygen levels get low enough to kill large numbers of fish) as a small, shallow lake.

In general, fishing gets "deeper and tougher" as midwinter wears on. But by locating fish and working them with live bait presentations, using a depthfinder as a "mood indicator" you can have better success now than most anglers do during the peak first-ice bite!

# In-Line Spinners for Smallmouth

When fishing for river smallmouths, I cast a 1/16-ounce in-line spinner quartering the current and reel in fast enough that the blade bulges the surface. Many people use this technique with spinnerbaits, but the smaller presentation of the in-line spinner calls the fish up when the larger lures fail. I use a black Wordens spinner with a silver blade. The strikes are viscious and rarely do the fish miss. Try it—you'll like it.

*Craig Henry*
*La Plata, MD*

# Put Ketchup on Your Spoon

I always keep a couple of small packets of ketchup in my tackle box to use as a polish for spoons and spinner blades. Just smear the ketchup on the lure, wait two minutes and then rub off. It's safe and environmentally friendly.

*Peter Fedra*
*Santee, CA*

# Add Shine to Crankbaits

When my favorite crankbaits get dull or scratched from teeth marks, I brush them with clear verathane or spar varnish. It makes them shinier than new.

*Denton Cramer*
*Rancho Murieta, CA*

# Double-Duty Fishing

I have found an easy and very effective way to fish for bass and panfish at the same time. All you need is a small floating Rapala, a small floating fly and about 14 inches of fishing line. Tie the fishing line to the tail end of the Rapala where the treble hook is attached to a ring. Tie the floating jig to the other end of the fishing line. To fish, reel in a line about a yard at a time, stopping for a few seconds. Continue until the lure is retrieved. You now have created a fish-catching monster.

*Jared Kiley*
*Cincinnati, OH*

# Glitter for Power Baits

I bait fish with Power Bait and have found that the glitter they add really does attract fish over the non-glitter type. So I bought some glitter from a craft store and added it to the the Power Bait. I simply take a ball of Power Bait and drop it in a plastic bag containing glitter. Then I shake the bag a little bit until the bait is covered in the glitter. When this bait hits the water, some of the glitter will come off and create a "puff" of glitter in the water. This attracts the trout to come and investigate. This method has doubled my catch. Now I don't go fishing without my bag of glitter!

*Kong Shang*
*Reno, NV*

# Crankbait Quick-Fixes

The one thing bad about crankbaits or minnow baits is that when you finally make a good cast, the line gets tangled around one of the treble hooks. Put a 1-inch piece of a coffee straw into the line before tying and it will be tangle free.

*Ray Lucas*
*Wesley Chapel, FL*

# Keep Your Fly Dry

If you're having trouble keeping dry flies from sinking, I have a solution. Bring some Vaseline or vegetable oil on your next trip and grease the line. It won't hurt the fish and it will keep dry flies on the surface.

*Anthony Bertrand*
*Lincoln, NE*

# Crafty Lures

I have improvised an inexpensive panfish grub lure from white or colored pipe cleaners. Wrap three or four turns of pipe cleaner around a plain lead head jig. A slight bend to the hook shank improves appearance and is even more effective when fish scent is allowed to soak into the fibers.

*Robert Kukuvka*
*Rockaway, NJ*

# Renew Your Lures

Over the course of a long fishing season and after years of use, crankbaits, spinnerbaits and minnow imitation lures become dingy, scratched or chipped. Fishermen are often tempted to replace lures. I recommend adding glitter to renew the lures appearance simply by utilizing waterproof glue or cement. It is easy and fun to customize your own lure and it's inexpensive.

*John Molla*
*Poway, CA*

# Reuse Old Worms

I fish with plastic worms and spinnerbaits a lot. When the plastic worms become no longer usable Texas style, I cut the tops off and use them on the spinnerbaits as trailers. If they are straight tail worms, I split the tail in half to get more action out of them.

*Allen Schoessow*
*Milwaukee, WI*

# Make-It-Yourself Treble Hook

Tackle shops sell "soft bait" treble hooks for about 50 cents apiece. They are easy to make at home for much less. Just take the springs out of cheap ball-point pens (or buy springs at a craft store), cut them to the length of the shank of a treble hook and slide it down the shank. Now pinch the last coil of the spring around the shank of the hook. Now you have a "soft bait" treble that is just as good as any bought in a store.

*Kong Shang*
*Reno, NV*

# Turbo Spinner

Before tying on a spinner or other bait, just slip a small prop and bead on the line. This creates extra flash, vibration and a turbulence of bubbles. Good all around, whether buzzing, free falling or just cranking.

*Steve Volz*
*Spokane, WA*

# Garlic for Bass

To add garlic scent to your soft-plastic baits, first go to the grocery store and buy a small jar of minced garlic. Put a teaspoon of the garlic into a bag of plastic worms. When you go fishing the bait will have the smell and taste of garlic that bass love.

*Victor Leake*
*Mannford, OK*

# Keep Your Eyes on This Lure

I use epoxy to glue on moving 3-D eyes on my weight-forward lures and jig heads. You can find them in most craft stores. They come in different sizes and colors.

*William Pugh*
*Cleveland, OH*

## Polished Lures

A simple and inexpensive way to customize your lures is to paint the lures with nail polish. This is great for when you're out on the water and your lure is just the wrong color. The polish only takes about five minutes to dry and comes in all colors of the rainbow and then some! There are also nail polishes that have sparkles in them for added flash.

*Mitchell Masuda*
*Salinas, CA*

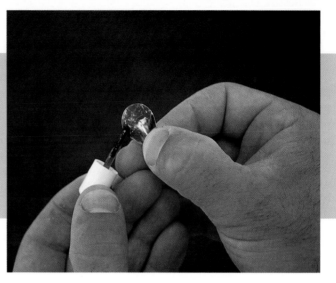

## Dyeing Spinnerbaits

I use this tip to add life to an old, chrome, dual-blade spinnerbait. First, dye the blades with some shotgun barrel bluing that you can purchase from your local ammo/gun store. You can use cotton swabs to apply the bluing; make sure you follow the directions on the bottle. To keep the bluing on, I apply some clear-coat epoxy on top of it. You'll now have a spinnerbait that will work great. If I'm fishing with spinnerbaits, I use my dyed spinnerbaits 99% of the time. I catch both bass and pike on them. You can also add a pork trailer to double your chances.

*Just Brinks*
*Wyoming, MI*

## Attracting Trout

Melt down Vaseline and add your favorite fish attractant to the mix. Once the Vaseline hardens, rub a light coat on your lure. I find these ideas most effective on trout.

*Justin Albert*
*Liverpool, PA*

## Float Flies Longer

For the trout fisherman, take some dry flies, and with scissors, cut some of the hackle off the belly of the flies. This will make the fly lay lower on the surface of the water and will make it more visible to the fish. It will also keep the fly floating longer since the hackle will be more dense and will repel the water more.

*Junior Martins*
*Garfield, NJ*

## Fire Up Your Baits

Are you tired of fish tearing up your soft plastics and crappie jigs? I have found a cheap, quick way to repair them. Simply take a match or lighter and apply the flame to the damaged part of the bait. The plastic will melt and cover the torn or damaged part. Then run under cold water to help the plastic harden faster. I have applied this method to some of my baits and have caught many more fish on them.

*Brandon Hutchinson*
*Mt. Vernon, IN*

# Crankbait Options

**I** mark the running depth on the bills of all my crankbaits with a green waterproof permanent marker. In addition, I keep three of each bait in my box: 1 tuned to run left, 1 tuned to run right and 1 tuned to run straight. I mark a small dot on the bill with the same marker to show which side the bait will run toward, leaving it blank if it is tuned to run straight.

*James Shunamon*
*Quincy, MA*

# Rattling Worms

**F** or easy insertion of rattles into plastic worms, insert a stiff coffee or cocktail straw into the area where the rattle should go. Then bend the end over to create a vacuum, then pull it out. The section of worm into which the straw was inserted should pull out along with the straw, leaving a nice hole into which you can insert the rattle.

*Justin Brinks*
*Wyoming, MI*

# Lipless Lures

**D** on't throw away your old floating minnow-type baits when the lips have broken off. You can break the lip completely off, sand and/or repaint the lure for use as a surface lure. Tie it on, cast it out and twitch it erratically across the surface much like a Spittin' Image Shad.

*Steve VonBrandt*
*Wilmington, DE*

# Fishing with Balloons

**D** on't throw away those balloons from the kid's birthday party—I cut them into various size strips and attach to the hooks of spinners and spoons—they have terrific action and the colors provide great variety.

*Robert Kukuvka*
*Rockaway, NJ*

## Snagless Spinnerbait

To avoid getting snagged while fishing a spinnerbait around grass, brush and other cover, take a rubber band and loop it around the line tie of the spinnerbait. Take the other end and hook it under the hook barb. It will help keep you from snagging, and the rubber band is flexible enough to allow a hook up.

*Coleby Gilliand*
*Deatsville, AL*

## Wet Worms

At one time or another everyone has had plastic worms get wet and milky colored. Don't throw them away, just lay them out on a piece of cardboard and they'll return to their original color.

*Steve VonBrandt*
*Wilmington, DE*

## Multiple Hook Rigs

I found that by using coffee can lids with holes poked in them, I keep my rigs longer lasting and have fewer tangles. I poke holes with a knife around the edges and then insert the hooks. I also cut the lids in half and use a hole puncher to make a hole to hang up my rigs after use.

*John C. Gallo*
*Uniondale, NY*

## Popping for Panfish

Most panfish anglers know how to use a popping bobber to attract panfish to their jigs, nymphs or streamers. However, it's just as easy and more productive to use a panfish popper instead of a bobber. The popper has both sound and color to attract fish and floats well enough to allow the submersed bait to swing forward and suspend. The tandem rig works well on ultra-light or fly fishing gear. Use a slow retrieve with short pops for inactive fish and a faster retrieve for more active fish. Active fish often strike the popper. When the popper pulls under or changes direction, you have a bite on the bottom bait, so set the hook and enjoy the fight.

*Michael Finley*
*North Hills, CA*

## Large Floating Jigs

I have always hunted around for larger than average floating jigs and could never find them. So, what I do now is I first find a long shanked hook in the size I need. I then get an appropriate size cork and thread the cork on the hook. Then I place a drop of glue and a little paint on it. Next thing you know, you're ready for fishing.

*Edward Pace*
*Factoryville, PA*

# Speed-Jigging By Trolling: Rip-Jigging

**D**ick Grzywinski knows about speed-jigging by trolling. "The Griz" is a regionally famous St. Paul, Minnesota, guide known for keeping customers on the water long after sunburn sets in. He's a top-flight angler who knows that fish aren't in the same spot every day. He likes the search. He calls it "rip jigging."

Before attempting it, read about it carefully. Even before that, wipe your mind's slate clean of everything you know about jig fishing. Forget every rule about presentation and boat control you've ever heard.

In short, what Griz does is troll forward along contours, weed edges or other likely areas. He casts a jig out as he's moving, a lot closer to the boat than you might think ("to heck with the thought that fish will spook from the boat").

Then, he settles in for a long day of snapping his wrist. Aggressively, he works his jig, a special homemade feather-duster he makes himself. You can quickly look over long shoreline breaks, large reefs and points and other large areas. Or, you can make a pass over a good spot, wheel around and come back through it. It's a great way to fish while you try to learn a new body of water.

It sounds simple, and it is. But like all simple, effective systems, there are small details that spell the difference between success and failure.

"The main thing," Griz says, "is to go out and do it, and experiment with getting the boat to move right. Boat control is very important.

Moving the boat right means:

* Motoring into the wind or current. This lets you control your movements easier, and lessens the change of moving too fast. Because he always moves forward, Griz doesn't have "splash guards" installed on his boat, a standard on most North-country rigs. He is comfortable in heavy seas that send many backtrollers to shore. To stabilize his movements in rough water, he tosses out a sea anchor that's tied on a short rope to the bow eye. "It keeps you moving straight, just like you're tied to a dock." (The short rope is critical, or the sea anchor could twist up in your motor.)

* Putting the boat over the precise depth that's holding the fish you want to catch. Fish often hold at definite depth zones which change from season to season and day to day. Once you catch a few fish at a certain depth, keep on that depth. On some days, deviating as little as 6 inches or a foot can mean no more bites, Griz maintains!

* Also, train yourself to notice the little things, like isolated hard-bottom areas in expanses of soft bottom, edges of weeds, the crest of a rock reef or sand point. Griz is practically world famous for catching tons of fish among other boats that are only picking up stragglers. "A lot of times," he says, "they don't realize that they're only a few feet from all the fish."

How heavy is the jig? He prefers a ¼-ounce feathered "Griz Jig" or Northland Fireball. But, he will use ⅛-ouncers in shallower water or when he wants to slow things down a bit.

How far should you cast out? Griz keeps the lure amazingly close. "In deeper water," he says, "you gotta be farther behind the boat. (He uses the method in water as deep as 25 feet, but average anglers would probably do best at 15 feet or less, especially while learning it.) It depends a lot on whether the water is clear or cloudy. In dirty water, or on real windy days, you can troll right over the fish and they'll still bite. But I'd say that most of the time I'm not more than 25 or 30 feet behind the boat. The jig drags on the bottom if you cast too far out."

(Try the rule of more line for clear and/or deep water; less for dirty and shallow, even if it seems that shallow fish would be spooky and would require a long-distance approach. Griz invented the method and wrote the rule book, and it works for him so it should work for you, too.)

How do you know how deep your jig is running?

Griz goes by 35 years of accumulated feel. With as much time as he spends on the water, that's like 245 dog years to you and me.

Mortals will have to experiment. Griz does not try to bounce the jig off the bottom to know where it is, but you might try that for awhile. Speed up a touch and assume you're just off. When the jig hits weeds, rip it again and it normally comes free. You can work this method through thick weeds and other cover that would stop slip-sinker rigs and crankbaits.

Should you tip it with live bait?

Griz likes fathead minnows. Any smallish, tough minnow should work well. Hook it through both eyeballs and it stays on the hook fairly well through the rigors of ripping.

How heavy should the line be?

Griz has settled mainly on 10-pound-test monofilament. "I'm ripping the jig so hard that I tear the line and break it all the time with 8-pound. I don't have any problems with 12-pound, but I like using 10-pound better. Still, I have to re-tie about every hour or even the 10-pound snaps off."

What kind of a jigging motion is it?

As for the "Rip" or the snap itself ... you guessed it ... it's all in the wrist.

"Get comfortable," Griz says. "I like to put my right leg up on my tackle box and get settled in. It's all wrist action. Don't use your arm or it drags the jig too much. You want that thing hopping around back there."

"Hold your rodtip down toward the water, and make a strong snap with your wrist, maybe about 3 feet forward. Don't raise your rodtip or it'll lift the jig too high. Snap your rod really quick forward, and follow the line back slowly so you can feel a hit."

Don't keep the line tight while you follow it back, or the jig won't sink and do its stuff. And, take heart if you're worried about being able to feel subtle strikes: You often hook the fish when you go to make the next wrist-snap! Instant hookset. It even happens to Griz sometimes.

It will feel strange to fish so close to the boat. (Through the years, Griz has found, especially in cloudier water, that he's able to fish as close as 8 feet behind the boat and catch fish in as shallow as 6 feet of water without spooking problems!)

Go farther back, especially in deeper and clearer water. But take in line or speed up if you're dragging bottom. Above all, when you first try this, ignore the little voices of reason in the back of your head. Because once you get the hand of "rip jigging," your smile may have to be surgically removed.

# Lure Color

I paint my blade lures flat black because I want the fish to see only the soft plastic part of my lure and the fish tend to eat the smaller looking portion of the lure.

Tim Laurila
Rockville, MD

# Lure Size

I found that "small catches all". The smaller lures are better at catching the different species at the same time. While bigger lures might limit you to one particular species. My best all-around pond lures are the medium-sized lures.

Tim Laurila
Rockville, MD

# Poor Man's Spinner Blade and Spoon Polish

A great way I found to bring back the shine to my copper and brass spinner blades is to cut a small slit into the side of a Taco Bell Hot Sauce packet and let the blade soak for about 20 minutes. Remove the blade and rinse with water and your blades will look like new! Try it with a penny. Don't laugh—it works!

Matthew Radzialowski
Wixom, MI

# Unique Plastic Worms

For a unique color scheme with plastic worms, create your own. Simply mix and match different color worms in a plastic bag. You can use a Ziplock or the bag that the worms came in. Leave the bag in the direct sunlight for a week or two. The colors will bleed together, yielding one-of-a-kind bass worms. Try both dark and light worms for some interesting results.

Martin Earhart
Charlotte, NC

# Killer Bass Lures

Take a lead head jig, hook on a worm, then take a tube bait and stick it over the jig and the worm.

Sean Merritt
Sugar Land, TX

# Weed Impeder

Spinnerbaits can be made weedless by using a small rubber band. Loop the rubber band around the line, tie and hook it up under the hook barb. It will stop weeds, but not fish!

Coleby Gilliand
Deatsville, AL

## Soak Your Baits

Try "soaking" your plastic baits in a jar of attractant overnight before a fishing trip. The baits will absorb most quality fish attractants. Just put in your plastic baits, apply a bit of scent and stir with a spoon before capping the jar.

*Jim Paige*

## Mixing Power Baits

I found that when using powerbait paste, often the basic colors are not what the fish want at that time. This is when it's time to roll a couple or several colors together, making your own rainbow mix. The biggest difference between bought and self prepared mixtures, is that typically you know what has worked so you can concentrate on more of these colors than the traditional blend. Experimentation will provide amazing results.

*Mark Nassis*
*Monroeville, PA*

## Spinning for Gar

Gar have long, toothy snouts. This can become an irritating problem when trying to hook one. A good, fool-proof way of landing one is by using a jerry-rigged spinnerbait. Take 2 or 3 feet of old, used monofilament off your reel and tie it to the hook of the spinnerbait. When the gar slashes at the bait, its teeth will get caught in the line. As it rolls on the surface, it will become even more entangled and trap itself.

*Coleby Gilliand*
*Deatsville, AL*

## Lures

To catch more largemouth bass and bluegills on spinnerbaits, cast out your line, then reel for 4 seconds, then stop for 2 seconds—continue to reel like that until you have to recast. You're sure to catch more!

*Drey Hawkins*
*Mountain View, OK*

## Accessorizing Jigs

I had this idea to either take off or leave on the skirt of a rubber skirted jig and hook a live or plastic crawdad through the tail. If you are using a plastic crawdad, the type with the tail that folds over works best. How do you fish this type of jig. Hop it along the bottom. It works well at night because that is when crawfish feed. Put some rattles on the jig for extra fish-attracting power. It also works to use pork rind or double-tailed worm instead of a crawdad. The jig needs to be heavy enough to stay on the bottom. Fish the worm and pork rind the same as a regular jig or hop it. You can also put cut bait or dip bait on the jig and let it sit there for catfish.

*Jeremy Williams*
*Fay, AR*

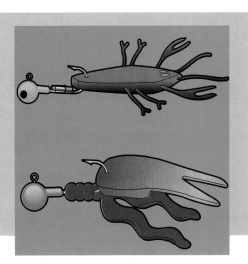

# Pretty Jig Heads

I take dull slipsinkers and jigheads and paint them with glitter nail polish ... you probably want to get your wife or girlfriend to buy the polish ... there are colors to match any worm or grub skirt. I use a Styrofoam base, sticking a toothpick into the Styrofoam to hold the weights to polish them. I also have another piece of Styrofoam with a small cut-out in the center, to hold the nail polish. This makes everyone extremely happy, as it eliminates spills.

*Denton Cramer*
*Rancho Murieta, CA*

# Watch Your Weight

When I get a new lure, I take a needle and somewhere on the bait I carve into it how much it weighs so that when I come back to the lure later, I still know how much it weighs.

*Sean Merritt*
*Sugar Land, TX*

# Inside Job

Instead of pouring fish attractant onto your favorite plastic bait, which can be messy and costly, use a worm blower or large-bore syringe to inject the scent into the plastic. Insert the tip of the needle into the bait and slowly inject the liquid. This will allow the scent to slowly escape instead of washing off.

*Steve Brown*
*Minneapolis, MN*

# Tune Up Your Spinnerbaits

Ever hear somebody say that "the fish are hitting the blade of my spinnerbait and they cannot get the hook"? The bait is probably running a little on its side. Spinnerbaits need to be tuned just as other lures do. Looking straight down on top of the lure, make sure that the line tie, blade connection and hook are in a straight 3-point alignment. If the bait still runs on its side, the blade may be too large for the speed of retrieve or the size of the lure body. The torque from the blade may be causing the bait to roll over. You can try slowing your retrieve, switching to a smaller blade, changing the blade style (Colorado, Indiana, willow) or adding a plastic trailer to stabilize the bait.

*Homer Lee*
*East Stroudsburg, PA*

# Wobbletail Lures

Here are the different sizes of wobbletail I use. ("Wobbletail" is a pending trademark.) Micro wobbletail uses a soft plastic crappie stinger. What makes these lures a challenge for fisherman to use is that you have to center the soft plastic after a fish strike pushes it down the hook. Also, the soft plastic has to be changed after being worn out catching fish. Lure action is ruined by using a snap swivel: It puts weight on top of the lure. I prefer to use a double loop knot. Line size also has an effect on wobble; that's why I use 4-pound test on micro wobbletail. The best color crappie stinger I have had success with is yellow/white.

I use the medium-sized wobbletail configured with a spinnerbait that has a #4 gold Colorado blade. I used the small 1½-inch Bass Assassin with this lure on the Monacacy River in Frederick, Maryland, to catch smallmouth and longear sunfish. Use only a 1½-inch Shad Assassin soft plastic with a topwater wobbletail lure. Bigger soft plastics that are re-rigged with this lure will cause it not to topwater "walk the dog" retrieve.

Large wobbletails are made with a ½-ounce blade. You can rig with a 6-inch straight soft plastic worm. This lure can be retrieved to make the worm resemble a snake swimming; it has a good thump as it is retrieved. All these lures, when fished, have the hook run up to be semi snag-resistant when retrieved.

A wobbletail swimming jig uses the 3-inch Slug-Go. This lure will show you how weight distribution effects a lure. This lure has no fins on the willowleaf blade, therefore it doesn't have maximum wobble movement. This is just a simple construction lure. Wire wrapping the hook eye is the most difficult part of the construction. You can go through the blade hole and tie directly to the hook eye to keep it more simple to use.

*Tim Laurila*
*Rockville, MD*

# Shine Up Your Spinners

Don't throw out old brass blades from your spinners and spinnerbaits when they get corroded and tarnished. If they are corroded, take a little steel wool to them. If they are just tarnished, use a little brasso to shine them up.

*Sean Merritt*
*Sugar Land, TX*

# Thumping Spinnerbaits

Do you want to make a spinnerbait thump and carry on? Take a single blade spinnerbait and open up the arms a little. Baits with Colorado blades work best for this. The bigger, the better ... within reason.

*Homer Lee*
*East Stroudsburg, PA*

# Add Bulk to Plastic Worms

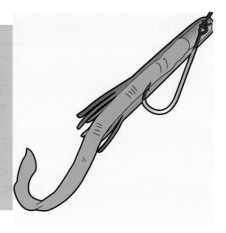

**P**ush the head of a plastic worm into the open end of a 3-inch tube bait. This allows you to mix and match colors as well as add "legs" to the middle of a 7-inch worm. Just Texas rig the set up and fish it as you would a regular worm.

*Brandon Radcliffe*
*Conyers, GA*

# Glow in the Dark

**I**f you want to power up glow-in-the-dark lures quickly and easily when on the boat, just use a powerful Mag-lite or spotlight. Turn the light to the sky and put the lure on top. In a few seconds (if the light is powerful enough) the lure should be shining brightly.

*Travis Pond*
*Grand Blanc, MI*

# Yankee Rig a Crankbait

**T**o yankee rig a crankbait, you need to tie a small to medium-sized dipsey sinker to the end of your line followed by a 3-way swivel 12 to 18 inches up the line. Tie the crankbait (large-lipped, deep divers work best) to the swivel with 6 to 7 inches of line. Cast and let settle to the bottom. With a swift motion, sweep the rod to your side. This will make the crankbait look like a feeding baitfish. This rig may be difficult to cast.

*Coleby Gilliand*
*Deatsville, AL*

# Entice Stubborn Bass

**H**ere is a tip for a special rig that I use for topwater fishing. It works great when the water is a little rough or even when the fish are just not very active. First, remove the back hook from a standard Hula Popper. Next, tie a short (5 to 10 inches) piece of fishing line to the base of the front hook (the small metal piece that holds the hook in place) and thread it up and through the back hook's eyebolt. Rig the other end of the line with a soft-plastic jerkbait such as a Slug-Go. I also sometimes replace the Hula Skirt with a plastic glitter skirt made for jigs. This rig will bring out stubborn bass, if for no other reason than to see what all the commotion is about. It really works!

*Justin Brinks*
*Wyoming, MI*

# Scented Spoons for Trout

Trout sometimes show interest in a spinner or spoon. They follow, but will not hit. Try this: Tie a piece of red yarn onto your hook—but first soak it with salmon egg scent. (Remove the scent soaked yarn before storing the lure ... it will promote rusting if left attached.) This is sometimes the extra incentive the fish need. I haven't tried other scents available.

*Homer Lee*
*East Stroudsburg, PA*

# Restore Shine to Spoons

To quickly restore the shine and/or remove tarnish from a silver or stainless spoon or other lure, just moisten your finger with some water and then pick up a cigarette ash or cold campfire ash. This mixture will form a paste that you can use to gently rub away the tarnish on the lure. Great for a quick shine when you're pressed for time.

*P. Carreras*
*Owingsville, KY*

# Use Wind to Your Advantage

Fishing in the wind can be frustrating. But you can use the wind to your advantage with this tip. When strong winds have your favorite lake looking like the North Sea, look for bluffs, cliffs or underwater structure that the wind/waves have been pounding against. Wind creates current that will pile up plankton and draw small baitfish. Bass will be there to feed on the concentration of bait. When the wind has been blowing the same for two or three days, you will increase the probability of finding a concentration of bass. To increase your ability to detect strikes in rough water, use a lead head jig rigged with a small plastic minnow or worm. Suspend this rig into the targeted area with a slip float. The wave action will lift your float/jig and impart all the action you could want. Keep a tight line and you can detect when you have a fish on despite the rocking of the boat.

*William L. McCabe*
*Napa, CA*

# Quick and Easy Lure Changes

When fishing for crappie, I tie on the end of my line a No Knot Fas Snap. When I want to change from a jig to a Mr. Twister, I just slide it off and put on whatever I want. It is easy and quick.

*Albert Rodzinak*
*Middlesex, NJ*

# Add Scent to Your Trolling Lures

**M**any trolling lures have hollow plastic bodies. You can add scent to these lures by drilling a hole (#40 drill) in the front of the lure and two smaller holes (#60 drill) at the back of the cavity. Use a precision oil injector or hypodermic needle to inject fish attractant into the cavity of the lure through the front hole. The pressure of the water at the front of the lure will push the attractant out of the cavity. The #60 sized holes will meter the amount of attractant released and reduce the number of refills required. Adding a scent trail to the flash and vibration will increase your effectiveness. On solid body lures or spoons, attach fish attractant paste to the swivel between your main line and the leader. Just form a tapered shape of the attractant around the swivel or attach a paste holding device (Little Stinker catfish bait company makes one) to produce the scent trail.

*William L. McCabe*
*Napa, CA*

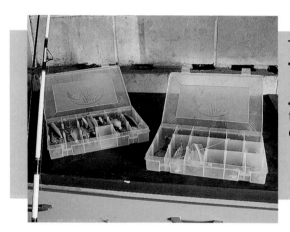

# Dry Out Lures

**K**eep your lures in top condition. When you return home from a day of fishing, make it a habit to leave your box of lures or book of flies open overnight so the contents can dry out. Moisture trapped in an airtight container will soon rust hooks and tarnish metal lures.

*Jason Hilton*
*Telford, TN*

# Bright Lures for Bright Days

**H**ere is a fishing tip that I find lucky for myself. On bright, sunny days I use bright colored lures. On low, cloudy days I use dark colored lures.

*Pinky Hewlett*
*Des Moines, IA*

# Modify a Jointed Stickbait

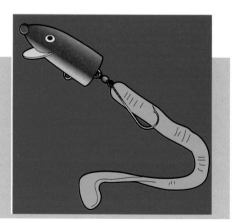

**R**emove the front treble hook and the back section of a jointed stickbait. Replace the back section with a split ring and a worm hook. Texas rig your favorite worm and fish through the grassbeds and floating vegetation.

*Brandon Radcliffe*
*Conyers, GA*

# Trailer Hooks Made Easy

Adding trailer hooks to spinnerbaits can make the difference when bass are striking short. You can use surgical tubing to hold the hooks in place, but the process is time consuming and the small pieces of tubing are hard to work with when in a boat. To avoid these problems, prepare your trailer hooks at home with this tip. Buy a tube of thick rubber shoe repair adhesive (Shoe Goo is one brand). Give the eyes of your trailer hooks a liberal coat of adhesive. Let it dry and give it a second coat. The hooks have a fixed rubber layer that will hold them in the correct position on your spinnerbait hook.

*William L. McCabe*
*Napa, CA*

# Shallow Fishing Strategies

When fishing for largemouth bass in shallow lakes or ponds, use a plastic worm and bump around the bottom with use of a 1/2-ounce sinker. Also, if there is a rock ledge, "swim" the worm up into that, hit the side a few times, and let it fall slowly back down. This will trigger strikes of annoyance or curiosity from any size of largemouth.

*Tracy Benton*
*Boca Raton, FL*

# Bucktail Shampoo

To eliminate the drying and stiffening of natural bucktails on your jigs and spinners, shampoo and condition them back to their original texture.

*Aaron Benes*
*Cambridge, MN*

# Paint Your Own Jigs

If you fish crappie around brush piles, you know losing jigs is a fact of life. To ease the sting of these losses a bit, buy unpainted leadheads for about half the price of painted ones. Cans of spray paint will last all year and you can paint all the leadheads you like (I use black and red). Painting your own leadheads will save you a chunk of change during the course of a fishing season.

*Jeff Ball*
*Richmond, VA*

## Floats for Tube Jigs

Insert a float into the back of the hollow body of a tubejig. This will help it stand on end.

*Ollie Wiitala*
*Dexter, MI*

## Purple Worms for Big Largemouth

My all-time favorite lure to use when fishing for largemouth bass is a plain purple worm. Many people find it to work better with a rig of some type, but I have caught 4-plus pounders on just a plain purple worm with the hook sticking out of the belly (or middle) and a 1/2-ounce sinker. Again, some people like to jig the worm once cast, but I caught my biggest bass ever by using just a quick but plain retrieve. Decide for yourself, but I'll keep my way.

*Tracy Benton*
*Boca Raton, FL*

## Bubbles for Bass

To attract bass and other gamefish, cut a small slit toward the back half of a plastic worm and insert a small chunk of seltzer tablet. When it hits the water, the tablet begins to fizz, leaving a trail of bubbles.

*Craig Shaloiko*
*Ruby, NY*

## Wide Wobble Lures

I found that I could catch more fish with a wide wobble. On my plain willowleaf lure I experimented with different spots to place the weight. Just a snap swivel weight on a small lure might "kill" the action of the lure.

*Tim Laurila*
*Rockville, MD*

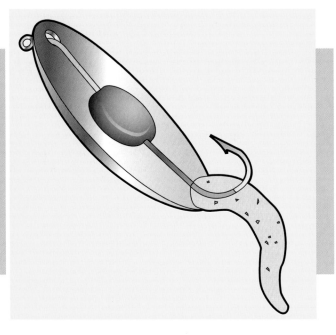

# Provoking Pike

I was pike fishing on the Chenango River from Greene to Binghamton, New York, and the fish just would not hook up on a lure. I then tried a 6- to 8-inch black rubber worm with two salmon hooks—one to hold the worm and the other as a stinger. I then clipped both to a snap swivel with no leader, deadly when doing a countdown, then I short twitched the rod. Pay attention to the bait as it makes northern pike very aggressive. I believe it's something in the speed of the twitch that triggers pike into this mode.

*David R. Zollbrecht*
*Greene, NY*

# Don't Re-tie That Line Again

When you are fishing for walleyes and the bottom is all rocks and stumps, don't get tired of hang-ups. I know a way that you don't have to keep on re-tying those lines. Tie a three-way swivel on your line, so it's connected onto your rod. Then on the other eye you tie your line with a floating jig head or something that will stay off the bottom. Then on the other eye you tie a line about a foot or so and attach a split-shot weight (put more if you need more weight). That way when you get hung up in a crack you just pull on your rod and the weights will just slide off. Then you don't have to keep re-tying that line all the time.

*Adam Sturm*
*Minnetonka, MN*

# Don't Destroy the Pork Frog

This tip involves removing pork frogs from the spinnerbait hook. Most people would snip or cut it off, but with trial and error, I've discovered a sure-fire way to remove them. What I do is take a coffee stirrer (the kind you get when you buy a cup of coffee), slide the stirrer over the barb and remove the plastic (or real) pork frog without destroying it.

*Christopher Thompson*
*Port Huron, MI*

# Better Rigging

Tired of getting short hits on plastic worms? Using an upholstery needle, thread your line through the center of the worm, starting at the head. About 2-inches from the tail, poke the needle out the side of the worm. Tie on the hook and rig Texas style.

*Dennis Glidden*
*Milwaukee, WI*

# Topwater Bait Teaser

You can change the action of topwater baits by adding a drop line and small jig or spoon to the rear hooks. The drop line should be about 8 to 12 inches. After making a long cast, reel the bait in with a steady retrieve, fast enough to bring the teaser up to the surface. Pause your retrieve. The weight/flutter of the falling teaser will activate your topwater bait. Many strikes occur at this point. Frequently, bass will strike the teaser as well.

*William L. McCabe*
*Napa, CA*

# Turn Down Your Eye Hook

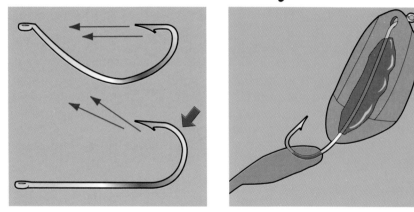

These are the reasons I prefer a hook with a turned-down eye:

1. Straight barb to eye hookset. Hook barb tends to pull outward.
2. On close examination this small curve hooks more fish than a wide gap hook. Fish have a tendency to feel the hook here. How many times do we eat with our mouths open all the way?
3. Curved hook sets into my blade.

*Tim Laurila*
*Rockville, MD*

## Fewer Snags

Here's a quick and easy way to help reduce the number of times your favorite crankbaits snag weeds, brush and rocks. Using a wire cutter or pliers, simply clip the lead (downward pointing) tine off each treble, especially the belly hook. Cut it close to the hook shank. The modification won't hurt the bait's action, but will allow it to slide over snaggy cover, instead of hanging up.

*Josh Miller*
*Austin, MN*

## Finesse for Bass

Make a slow-falling plastic worm by threading it onto an $1/8$-ounce (or lighter) ballhead or mushroom jigs. Hook should be exposed. Good finesse tactic for finicky bass.

*Kurt Beckstrom*
*Managing Editor, North American Fisherman*

## Short Hit Success

Tired of missing those short hits with plastic? After inserting the hook through the front of the plastic minnows, I attached a treble hook, then an appropriately sized "o" ring, then completed the rigging of the hook through the body of the plastic—no more missed "short hits".

*Allen L. Clemons*
*Pope Valley, CA*

## Super Solution

I've found a way to temporarily hang your favorite lures and jigs within easy reach, in any boat or canoe. Use a strong, quick-drying glue to fasten short strips of $1/2$-inch thick foam to the side of the hull next to your boat seat. When fishing, hang the most frequently used lures beside you on the strip by pushing the hooks into the foam. You won't have to go through your tackle box every time you change lures.

*Tim McGarvey*
*Croydon, PA*

## Uni-to-Uni Knots Build Instant Leaders

If you fish superlines, but still prefer the convenience and invisibility of mono at the lure, use the simple-to-tie uni-to-uni knot to add one to 10 feet of leader.

*Steve Pennaz*
*Executive Director, North American Fisherman*

## Trophy Bass and Rubber Baits

Are you tired of having your trophy bass take a bite out of your rubber bait? I got tired of the same old problem, so I decided to do something about it. I tied up two hooks on one line. I string the hook on the end down through the middle of the bait to the tail. I stick the other hook in the head of the rubber bait. This seems to work exceptionally well in weedy bass ponds.

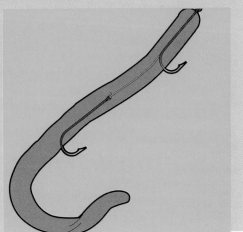

*Luke Beaucage*
*Friendship, ME*

## Scent Solution

Can't get your favorite scent to stay on your lure? All you need are a dozen pipe cleaners from your local craft store, a plastic Ziploc bag and your favorite scent. Cut the pipe cleaner into 1-inch sections, place them in the bag, and squirt them 5 to 8 times with scent. Close the bag, let it sit overnight and by morning your new "scent strips" will be ready to wrap around a hook or jig body. It's an inexpensive way to play the scent advantage.

*Daniel Marlowe*
*Ellicott City, MA*

# Hook-n-Lure Protection

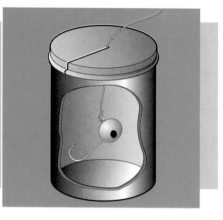

Take a 35 millimeter film canister, cut a slot from the center of the lid to the outer edge. Then place hook, small lure and jig inside canister. Slip line through slot and snap lid. There you have it.

*Stephen Turnis*
*Dubuque, IA*

# Allow Your Bait to Move

If you're fishing a crankbait without a split ring attached to the pull point, use a round-nose snap or a loop knot to allow the bait freedom to move. Otherwise you'll inhibit its action. About the only time you want a snug knot is when you want to increase the bait's roll. Then use an improved cinch knot snugged slightly below the bait's horizontal axis.

*Dan Johnson*
*Senior Editor, North American Fisherman*

# Assemble Your Own Spinnerbaits

Have you seen that new spinnerbait, two blades, each off swivels? I have been assembling my own baits for a couple years. Every time the blades contact each other, they make noise. They stutter and change rotation and speed. The swivels allow the blades to start whirling again and that little overlap allows them to hit again! They must overlap a little bit when the blade is in the retrieve position. Use top quality ball bearing swivels. Use clear plastic tubing from a fly shop, the kind of tubing used for tube flies. You must use the tubing to keep the blades and swivels spaced so they don't tangle. If you make your bait correctly, the blades should not be able to tangle with other lure components.

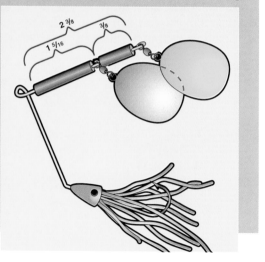

Approximate dimensions:
A. Total arm length: 2³/₈-inch
B. Tubing: 1⁵/₁₆-inch
C. Tubing: ³/₈-inch

*Homer Lee*
*East Stroudsburg, PA*

## Weedless Timber Jigs

**W**hen probing brushy cover for crappie, use a jig with a light-wire hook. With a pliers, bend the hook shank down at about a 45-degree angle, then Texas rig your plastic grub or twister tail trailer, leaving the hook point buried in the plastic. This will reduce the number of snags you get, increasing the number of slabs you catch.

*Steve Pennaz*
*Executive Director, North American Fisherman*

## Check Your Action

**W**hen trolling a crankbait, always start the troll by dropping the lure into the water at boatside and checking the action. Make sure the boat speed is right to create the action you want to give the lure. Then slowly pay out the line rather than casting the lure back behind the boat. This way, you'll know the lure is running true and didn't get fouled on the cast. Of course, you should still check the bait periodically to make sure it hasn't become fouled with weeds or sunken leaves.

*Dan Johnson*
*Senior Editor, North American Fisherman*

## Mark Your Crankbaits

**I** always thought it was a pain and a waste of space to keep my crankbaits in their original packaging when I put them in my tackle box. Problem was, whenever I threw away a lure box, I also lost the manufacturer's information on its running depth. Then I started writing the running depth details, such as "1.5 mph, 10-pound mono, 25 feet," on the belly of each lure in permanent marker. Now my crankbaits are easier to store and use than ever before.

*Walter Raven*
*Oakdale, MN*

# Where Do You Find Trophy Bass?

**M**ost flowages offer numerous "holes" carved out by the currents or created by small sinkholes. Bass fishing success in these depressions can be significant. An obvious surface key to locating structure in rivers is the bends. Contrary to some beliefs, creek and stream depths vary greatly, depending on where you are looking. Outer bends offer the most current and are generally the deepest part of a waterway.

On slow-moving tributaries, the outside bends are usually where big bass live. The successful shiner fisherman must pick those spots with the best big-bass potential. In stained waters, the areas should have at least 4- or 5-feet of water present with some form of cover, according to Bob Stonewater, largemouth bass expert. A deep creek flowing into or out of an even deeper channel is ideal. Even a 4-foot-deep outlet with flowage only during high water periods can hold a big fish if the cover is sufficient.

"People won't go into places that are only 10 feet wide," Stonewater explained. "Lunker bass will, though, because it's the depth of water and amount of current that's most important, not the width of the creek. You'll catch them on natural bait, too."

"Big bass search for such spots to lay out of the current and feed," he continues. "Water no wider than 15 feet or so can be eight feet deep and offer a sharp, sloping shoreline that big bass like."

Stonewater guided me to one such place on a recent trip. The ditch was actually a main river fork that only flowed during relatively high waters. The small channel is actually dry in some places during normal water levels. The guide was right about there being big bass present that day. We caught four bass from 6 to 8½ pounds drifting huge shiners along the bank.

Stonewater was familiar with that spot, but I've seen him analyze other spots with which he had no previous experience and draw the correct conclusion regarding their harboring big bass. On another abbreviated fishing trip using shiners one year earlier, we had two largemouths of bragging size. Together, they weighed more than 17 pounds and came from similar locations, miles apart!

Patience comes into play when waiting on a giant bass to feed. It may eat a mouthful and not feed for another whole day. Large bass feed primarily on big items such as golden shiners when an opportunity presents itself. Since it is difficult to predict when the fish will feed, a successful angler may have to work a prime spot four or five times during the day. Sooner or later, the large predator will probably move to her feeding grounds.

Repeated casts with lively shiners are often necessary to entice a large bass to strike. If the depth, current and cover are right, there will be a big bass feeding there at some time.

"My dad fishes holes where he'll sometimes make 40 or 50 casts," says Stonewater. "Many times he'll catch an 8-, 9- or 10-pound bass on the last cast! Knowing what cover has the potential to hold the big feeding bass is the key."

Throughout they day, Stonewater will verify depths with his 7-foot rods by poling downward through stained water to reach the bottom. If the tip touches just before the reel is submerged, the affable 45-year-old will call that "reel deep." And that is potentially deep enough for the lunker bass he's after.

## Increase Spinnerbait Vibration

**T**o give your willow-leaf spinnerbait a touch more kick (for more vibration), bend the last 1/2-inch of the blade 90 degrees downward. More vibration than a regular willow-leaf, less than a Colorado.

*Kurt Beckstrom*
*Managing Editor, North American Fisherman*

## Stop Sliding Worms

**I** fish plastic worms a lot and I've always been frustrated at how the bait gets pulled out of place down the hook by heavy vegetation. Now I have a solution. Tie a piece of stiff monofilament fishing line on the hook shank where it first comes out of the head of the worm and heads down the body. Twist the line about 5 times, so it's close to the body of the worm (fewer snags). Now the worm won't slide down the hook as easily. I've found this works much better than using glue to keep the plastic in place on the hook.

*Joe Parks*
*Loma Linda, CA*

## Slug-Gos for Largemouth

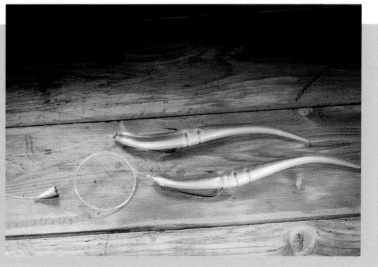

**I**n water 6 inches to 3-feet deep, I use a 6-inch Slug-Go without weight. In deeper water I use the same bait with an 1/8-ounce bullet sinker pegged about 18 inches up the line. My favorite colors are grape, root-beer and black-and-gray. Finally, don't forget to cast Slug-Gos into eelgrass and lily pads, where largemouth are often waiting to ambush an easy meal.

*Henry Petisca*
*Fall River, MA*

# Dishwater Lures

**A**s I was getting my fishing gear ready for the season, I discovered that a bottle of liquid fish attractant had spilled in the bottom of my bass box. All my jigs and skirted spinners were saturated. I thought about fishing them that way, but decided I had to clean up the terrible mess. I was trying to wipe and rinse the attractant off, to no avail, when it occurred to me to try the dishwasher. All the lures went right in the silverware holder and came out looking like new. Next time you want clean lures, throw them in the dishwasher!

*Dennis Jansen*
*Kimberly, WI*

# Jig Heads and Flies

**O**ne of the big things these days is trout flies with jig heads. Use a shortcut—tie feathers, etc. on ice jigs.

*Richard Richter*
*Michigan City, IN*

# Noisy Baits for Noisy Waters

**I**n calm water, I use plastic worms, jigs and topwater lures. In rough water, I use crankbaits, spinnerbaits or—in other words—noisy baits.

*Pinky Hewlett*
*Des Moines, IA*

# Far Casting Surface Baits

**G**et more casting distance out of hollow plastic surface baits—slit the back of a hollow plastic bait and fill with ¹/₂-inch chunks of plastic worm. More casting weight, yet it still floats.

*Kurt Beckstrom*
*Managing Editor, North American Fisherman*

# Dyeing Worms

**I**nstead of buying a bunch of dyes for my plastics, I just take a lighter-colored worm that you want to dye and stick it in with other worms of a different, darker color. If it doesn't work, stick a little worm oil in with them.

*Sean Merritt*
*Sugar Land, TX*

# Light Tackle for Panfish

An ol' timer in the high country of Colorado showed me a method that I have used very successfully on beaver ponds and almost any kind of still water. Sometimes fish seem to be hitting only insects on the surface, such as mid-mornings or late afternoons and your usual spinning gear just isn't doing any good. Try putting a clear plastic bobber on the end of your line. Attach a fairly long leader, 4 or 5 feet, of very light 1- or 2-pound-test mono. Tie on 2 dry flies if you're rich, or a wet fly treated with line dressing if you're like me. The idea is for the fly to float. Cast out. The bobber is the weight. In a few seconds, begin to reel in slowly enough so that the bobber makes no wake. This works well on trout, pond bluegill and other brim. With the light tackle, you really have to work these super fighting panfish. A few flies and some clear bobbers don't take much room in your tackle box and you'll be prepared for those occasional opportunities.

*Tom W. Ross*
*Miami, FL*

# Effective Jigs

To enhance the effectiveness of a plain jig, attach a snap and swivel with spinner blade on snaps. Slip this swivel over the hook—you might have to squeeze down the barb of the hook with pliers if the swivel eye is too small. Cut out a disk from a plastic lid of a coffee can and slip this over the hook to retain spinner assembly. I have added this small marabou crappie jig with outstanding success.

*Robert Kukuvka*
*Rockaway, NJ*

# Add a Stinger to Your Rat-L-Trap

Hook the eye of a light-wire hook onto the eye (not the split ring) of your Rat-L-Trap. Then shape and super glue the hook to the back of the lure. The line will keep the weeds off the hook.

*Brandon Radcliffe*
*Conyers, GA*

# Spoon Revival

To get rid of corrosion, rust and scum accumulation on your spoons, place the items in a plastic bowl, throw in a hand full of beach sand, put the lid on and shake. After a few minutes the green corrosion, rust and dull scum is gone. Rinse with fresh water, sharpen the hooks and apply a coat of silicone.

*Donald Crain*
*MM2 US NAVY*

# Cruising Bass

A tip I have is to use surface lures at night. Bass cruise the surface when the moon is out. I guess they are attracted to the light.

*Jeff Swarthout*
*Barryton, MI*

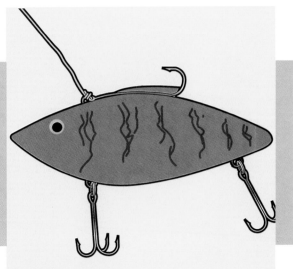

# 3

# BAITS

**B**ait fishing doesn't mean just suspending a gob of worms below a bobber anymore. What's more, using live or natural bait is often just the best way to catch some fish, period. Bottom line? Bait is great! And NAFC members — no strangers to successful bait fishing — are ready and willing to share their secrets and insights right here.

# Minnow Rig

**W**hen fishing a minnow jig, more often than not I will rig the minnow the following way: The hook should go in the mouth and then out the gill. The minnow is then slid up the hook so it is "kissing" the jig head. To keep the minnow "kissing" the jig head, I then bend the minnow slightly and run the hook up the belly and out the back. This rigging makes it easier to fish the weeds and puts the hook further back on the minnow to catch short-strikers. It does kill the minnow much quicker than other rigging options, but the fisherman has more control over the lure and can deliver his own action through an aggressive jigging action.

*Sean Gohman*
*Waconia, MN*

# Peg Sinkers Successfully

**M**y son discovered a great way to peg sinkers without damaging the line. All you need is a 1-foot section of fishing line and a "stopper." You can use either a rubber band or flexible skirting from a jig. Rig your plastic worm and sinker as usual. Then, slide both ends of the 1-foot line through the sinker and put the stopper in the resulting loop. Pull both the tag ends until the stopper begins to come through the sinker, then let go of one tag end and pull the line out. Trim the stopper and slide the sinker down to the bait.

*Arlene Blandi*
*Renton, WA*

# Enticing Worms

**I**f you want to make your live worms more enticing, soak them in beet juice overnight. In the morning, take them out and catch some fish.

*Scott Sewall*
*Hillsboro, TX*

# Versatile Sinker

**F**or a versatile no-snag bottom-bouncer type sinker to be used for drifting or trolling for walleye or catfish, I use a three-way swivel. Then on the dropper use very heavy mono 6- to 8-inches with a knot tied to the bottom. Clamp on split-shot sinkers evenly spaced from bottom to top, as many as it takes to keep it on the bottom. More current or depth calls for more or heavier sinkers. Then, to keep the works from snagging, slip over it an equal length of surgical tubing and peg it to the hole in the three-way swivel. This rig works great—keeping your amount of tackle to the minimum because it is so versatile and changeable.

*Stephen Turnis*
*Dubuque, IA*

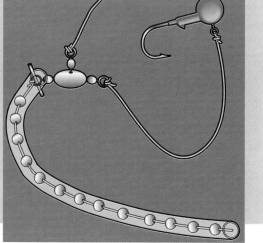

## Bad Bass Bites

Have you ever had a bass bite at the sinker? Add a short line with a worm.

*Jeff Swarthout*
*Barryton, MI*

## Perch for Perch

Perch swim in schools, therefore you want to cast to the same spots as quickly as possible after a good strike. A good bait to use for this (where legal) is to take a perch, cut it open, and cut a strip of stomach lining ¼-inch by 2 inches long, bait it on a small, thin bait holder hook and it will last for many bites.

*Jeremy Gooch*
*Sturgis, MI*

***Editor's note: Check with your state's regulations to see if this practice is legal in your state.

## Worm Action That Bass Love

To give a bass worm more action, take a utility knife and cut the back 2 inches into 4 to 8 strands. It gives the worm incredible action that bass can't resist.

*Jeremy Gooch*
*Sturgis, MI*

## Long-Lasting Doughballs

If you like to fish for cats with doughballs, here's a tip that can save you money. Put your doughball on the hook like usual. Then, take a small piece of nylon hose and put it around the doughball. Fasten the nylon hose onto the line using a small rubber band. This will help your doughballs last longer, while allowing the scent to still be released. This is extremely effective in the warmer rivers down south, where the doughballs tend to fall off the hook after a short while.

*Reed Gunter*
*Chapin, SC*

## High Floater

When Carolina rigging, take a hypodermic needle and inject air into your bait. This will make it float higher in the water.

*Coleby Gilliand*
*Deatsville, AL*

# 5-Gallon Crayfish Trap

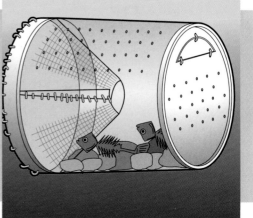

**F**orm an old window screen into a cone and place it into a 5-gallon bucket. Hold the cone together by using twist ties making sure you leave a 2-inch opening at the bottom of the cone. Drill 1/8-inch holes around the rim of the bucket and attach the screen to the bucket using twist ties. Cut an access hole into the rear of the bucket, and re-install using twist ties for hinges (you will need a 1/2-inch hole for this). Drill 1/8-inch holes all over the bucket to help it sink. Fill the bottom of the bucket with rocks and fish heads from the access hole.

*Matthew Radzialowski*
*Wixom, MI*

# Avoid Double Rig Hook Tangles

**W**hen using a double rig hook and floating bait, some anglers tie two hooks to two separate leaders of different lengths. This allows you to fish at two different depths at the same time. But the leaders often get tangled during hook sets and fish battles. This is really frustrating to me. Instead, I use an in-line leader formation. I tie a short leader to one hook and tie my next leader to the bend of that hook. I still get to fish at two different depths and have no more tangles. Be sure to use a fine diameter leader.

*Kong Shang*
*Reno, NV*

# My Favorite Catfish Set Up

**P**ut a large split-shot about 8 inches above a size 5/0 hook. Then put a float that can slip above that. Then hook a small bluegill through the back (1-2 inches). I have caught numerous channel cats off this rig.

*Brandon Radcliffe*
*Conyers, GA*

# Finding Giant Cats Through the Seasons

When searching for big catfish, Bob George, catfish guide, stresses the importance of finding a lake that has a history of producing exceptional sized fish. NAFC members should consult their state fishery department, local F.I.N. affiliates, wardens and biologists to ferret out these top spots for lunker cats.

Once you have selected a body of water, purchase a topographic map of the lake and study it to find possible catfish hangouts. Then go out in your boat and locate those spots with the depth finder. Search for actual fish, too, which will appear as large inverted U's or V's on a graph or thick bands on a flasher, on or near the bottom.

In spring large catfish often move into surprisingly shallow water, according to George. "I've caught huge ones in as little as 3 feet of water in March and April," he said. "Other times they might be as deep as 12 feet." Long, sloping points, flats, bars, old roadbeds and shallow, flooded timber all are worth prospecting for spring catfish. Anchor and cast to the area where you expect fish to be, put the rods in their holders and wait. When a fish takes the bait, give him a few seconds, then set the hooks with a hard sweep of the rod.

As the water warms up in summer, look for big cats in deeper water where the fish seek out their preferred temperature range and better oxygen supplies. Shallows still can produce a flurry of action early and late in the day, but for the most part, deep water is the payoff zone for the largest summer catfish. Depths of 20 to 60 feet are optimum, according to Bob.

But depth is only part of the formula. "Old flooded bridges, canals, roadbeds, buildings, cemeteries, sharp drop-offs, holes, timbered bars, anything rough—that's what a big cat will hold around," George said. "They seem to like tall structure, like a wall on a flooded building or canal. When the depthfinder lights up red for a 10- to 15-foot span, you're on top-notch cat cover!" A uniformly flat bottom that suddenly drops off 5 or 10 feet into a hole is another choice spot for finding jumbo summer catfish.

## Simple Trout Tactics

I feel that getting key hints on fishing is very important! I am going to tell you my secret on how to catch nice, big, luscious trout. I take a worm and put it on the hook. Then I add a little ball of power bait. When I first experimented with this technique, I caught a 12-inch trout on my first cast.

*Morgan Arnold*
*Oregon City, OR*

## Free Bait

Take a greasy piece of paper and a fly swatter with you when fishing. Swat your bait as needed.

*Richard Richter*
*Michigan City, IN*

# Try This Successful Rig

I have had huge success with this rig on lake or stream. I use the clear torpedo bubble with a ³/₁₆-inch hole drilled through to sink and cast with distance. Any type bait can be used; trailing approximately 18 to 24 inches behind the bubble. The bubble attracts fish while moving the bait behind.

*Tom P. Hoffman*
*Pottsville, PA*

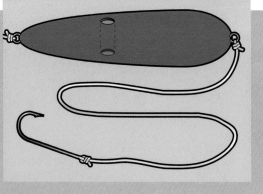

# Carp Dough Recipe

½ cup brown sugar
2 cups cornmeal
½ cup flour
1³/₄ cup molasses
canned corn liquid or water

Combine brown sugar, cornmeal, flour and molasses. Mix thoroughly then add corn liquid or water (whichever you choose to use) until a stiff dough is formed. Chill if a stiffer dough is desired. This recipe is also good for catfish.

*Robert Owens*
*Baltimore, MD*

# Big Bass Rig for Deep Water

Everyone knows that a pig and jig is a great deep water bait for big bass. You can add vibration and action to this lure by rigging a floating jerk bait in conjunction with the jig. Pass the line through the eye of the jig and tie on a swivel. Add a 3- to 4-inch leader and a floating jerk bait. Make your cast and give your line some slack (1 to 3 feet). The jerk bait will float up with the slack line. With a snap of your rod, the jerk bait dives to the jig looking like a small fish harassing a crawfish. The jerk bait sends out vibration and flash attracting bass within visual and lateral line range. If the bass are feeding on crawfish, they can choose the jig. If bait fish are on the menu, the jerk bait gets the call.

*William L. McCabe*
*Napa, CA*

# Long-Lasting Attractant

To keep the fish attractants from washing off your bait, slide a small piece of sponge onto a hook and then dip it into the attractant and let the sponge soak some up.

*Lee Jones*
*Davie, FL*

# Add Scent and Action

**M**y tip is something that I learned from an old Indian guide 30-plus years ago in Northwest Ontario. One natural way to add scent and action to a jig is to cut the bottom portion of skin from underneath a walleye's jaw (obviously, you do this to a walleye you are keeping to eat). This creates a natural "V" shaped chunk of fresh fish flesh. Insert the jig hook in the pointed end of the "V" and you'll have a natural, tough, scented jig trailer.

*Wayne Kottman*
*Lexington Park, MD*

\*\*\*Editor's note: Check with your state's regulations to see if this practice is legal in your state.

# Catching Bait Fish

**T**ake a 2- to 5-gallon can or jug with a large screw on lid. Cut 2 angle slots in the large removable lid 3 to 6 inches long, 1¹/₂ to 2¹/₂ inches wide, large enough for Wild Shiner's or bait to enter. Bait unit with a can of cat food. Cut small holes in food can. Release food at your discretion. Hang the large can (jug) off your dock. Bait or wild shiners can be harvested at your discretion. Use, save or sell the bait. Chum area over large can for better results. You can cast a net over the area after short term results. This makes excellent largemouth bass or catfish bait.

*Captain A.C. "Andy" Lowe*
*Satsuma, FL*

# Straighten Out Your Leeches

**I**n most cases, leeches tend to ball up on jigs and don't want to swim. To prevent this, slide a short piece of surgical tubing over the collar of the jig. Hook the leech far enough ahead of the sucker so the sucker can attach to the tubing. Leeches that attach themselves to something are less likely to ball up.

*Nick Waszczak*
*Des Planes, IL*

# Bait for Bait

**C**atch crickets for bait. Crickets make excellent bait for bass and panfish, and bread and sugar make excellent bait for crickets. Sprinkle the bread with sugar, slightly moisten, and leave the bread on the ground overnight beneath a cloth or newspaper. You'll collect a day's supply of bait.

*Jason Hilton*
*Telford, TN*

# Unusual Bass Bait

An excellent bait for bass is a live moth hooked through the body. It flutters on the surface and attracts bass. They can't resist it. It will get them everytime.

*Jeff Swarthout*
*Barryton, MI*

# Catfish Bait

If you want to catch catfish and you don't have any bait around, mix some flour and water together. Add some crushed dog food or crushed cat food in with the flour and water. Mix it until it forms a thick dough. Pull pieces off, roll them in balls and fish with them.

*Bryan Owens*
*Bolivia, NC*

# Dog Food for Cats

A great bait for channel catfish and large carp is Purina Dog Chow. It's cheap, easily transportable and easy to use. Just put 10 to 20 pieces in a container, cover with water for one to two minutes and drain. Use a #1 or 100 gold wire Mustad hook and push into the chunk of dog food. You can use a weight, but I've had the best results free floating it. The dog food will leave a visible "slick" in the water. It's inexpensive, easily transportable, not messy or smelly, and can be used as chum.

*Randy Jacobs*
*Lubbock, TX*

# Shrimp for Cats

A catfish angler will find this tip interesting. Frozen, uncooked shrimp make an awesome bait. Take only the middle part of the shrimp and put the hook through it. Use a 1-ounce sinker just above the hook. Cast out as far as you can; a cove is the best area to attempt for catfish. Leave the bait alone and prop the rod up. Eventually, a catfish will bite. This technique works quite well. I have caught a 17-pound catfish on shrimp.

*Tracy Benton*
*Boca Raton, FL*

# Still Catfish Rig

This rig works great on the Santee-Cooper lakes. Use #4 trebles with chicken liver and corn. Use #4 trebles with shad and nightcrawlers, along with a 1- or 2-ounce sinker.

*Tripp Ford*
*Piedmont, SC*

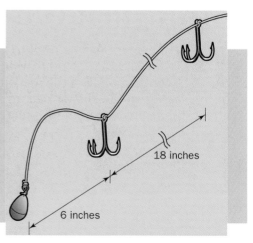

18 inches

6 inches

# Leeches—Gathering, Care and Maintenance

Preserving leeches is as easy as stashing them in buckets in a bait refrigerator. Side-by-side coolers—one for leeches, the other for minnows—on the top shelf with room for other baits below offers an ideal setup.

A season's worth of leeches can also be stored in an inexpensive, water-filled Styrofoam cooler placed in a cool, shaded spot. Divide the storage containers in half with a window screen to separate ribbon and tiger leeches, or large and small leeches. It's much easier to segregate them in the comfort of your garage than in a boat.

Wide-mouth, gallon glass jars filled with water work, too. Half-gallon plastic milk cartons hold fewer leeches; however, they pack so well in the refrigerator that you may be able to store more bait in them than in larger, bulkier containers. Using several small containers also makes it easier to determine when any leeches turn suckers up. If kept in clean, unchlorinated water under 50 degrees and checked once a week to remove dead and dying specimens, leeches caught in the spring should survive all summer without food. (They just shrink a bit.) Feeding small amounts of sliced liver to the leeches will head off this shrinkage, but some feel the enforced fast improves the leeches' texture. Also, because they're hungry, they seem to wiggle more vigorously on the hook.

Remember that chlorine kills leeches, so use unchlorinated water, such as rainwater or well water, or buy pills at the pet store to remove chlorine. At the end of the season, return the leftover leeches to their pond.

Spring is the best time to gather leeches because of the large number of "pre-spawn" adults. In the warm waters of summer, leech numbers decline because adults die after leaving the cocoons that hold the next year's leech population. Summer collection is possible, but just not that productive in most waters. This is why it's difficult to store leeches at home during winter.

Good collection spots for leeches include farm ponds, back-waters, ditches and other waters heavily overgrown with shoreline vegetation. Keys to finding large leech populations include a big summer algae bloom, the absence of gamefish and a little current to spread the scent of decomposing bait.

Many anglers look for leeches in ponds with large populations of fathead minnows. The minnows die in the spring after spawning, providing copious leech fodder. Again, the best spots within such habitat include places where a slight current moves the smell of your bait to leeches. Double up with crayfish or minnow traps and collect a smorgasbord of baits during one trip.

Collecting a season's supply of leeches is easy in the spring when water temperature reaches the magic 50-degree mark and leeches can swim into the traps. The most common leech trap is probably a coffee can in which the sides have been crimped down over some liver or other bait. Punch a hole in the top of the can and attach a small float. (Some anglers use Styrofoam balls; but less-trusting types use small sticks that attract less attention.) Ten- to 12-can traps improve chances of getting enough bait.

A baited gunnysack works well, too. Leeches can squeeze through the loosely woven fabric. Use dead animals found on the road for bait. It's also possible to get leeches to attach themselves to submerged boards. A board soaked in fish oil and then submerged near the bank overnight can attract a lot of leeches too.

If using the right container, you can encourage the leeches to sort themselves. For example, horse leeches have strong suckers enabling them to climb the sides of a minnow bucket or Styrofoam box. If you stash your holding box in shallow water overnight, the horse leeches will most likely leave, eliminating the nasty sorting process.

# A Different Way to Hook a Minnow

A wise old man from Birchwood, Wisconsin, once told me how to bait a hook with a minnow and I would like to pass it on to my fellow sportsmen. Hooked in this way, the minnow will stay alive much longer while still fishing. The hook is pointed in the right direction to catch most attacking fish. Just put the hook through the skin on the dorsal fin (facing forward). The minnow will swim wounded, but not harmed like if it were stabbed under the fish from side to side.

*Stephen Turnis*
*Dubuque, IA*

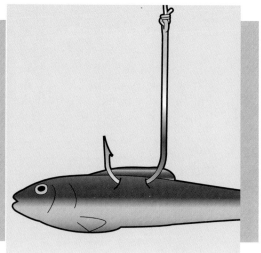

# River and Stream Presentations

You can either move your bait in an effort to put it in front of your targeted quarry or let it stay put so fish can follow its scent up to the hook. The decision hinges upon the activity level of the fish you are seeking.

When fish are in a migratory mode, such as salmon or steelhead hiding behind rocks or in deep pools, consider "plonking" or simply chucking your bait into the water and waiting for the action to develop.

Most still-water bait rigs work in holes. When minnows are fished in one spot in current, they should be lip-hooked; tail- or dorsal-fin hooked minnows tend to spin and twist the line. However, you should fish a minnow off a Wolf River or breakaway dropper setup in current so it spins attractively; a ball-bearing swivel reduces line twist.

# Ode to Daily Limit

An effective (and inexpensive) fish attractant can be made from dead shad. Take the shad and put them in a widemouth mason jar (don't forget to put a lid on it!) Take the jar and put it on your roof until the shad have become liquefied. This usually takes about a week depending on the temperature.

*Coleby Gilliand*
*Deatsville, AL*

# Moths for Bait

Got a bug catcher? The bag kind, not the zapper, works with a fan that sucks the bugs into a bag. Raid it for the weirdest collection of moths you ever saw to use as bait.

*Richard Richter*
*Michigan City, IN*

# Slugs for Bait

Slugs make good panfish bait. They stay on the hook very well. Use them up to 3/4 inch for panfish and bigger ones for catfish.

*Richard Richter*
*Michigan City, IN*

# Saltwater Tactics

For those of you who like to fish saltwater, I have a technique that has caught more than its fair share of fish. First, take a shrimp and cut in half. Throw away the head part; it has no use. Take your hook and run it all the way through the tail, coming out between the "fan of fins" at the very back, so that it appears as if the tail is held onto the end of the fishing line as if by some miraculous reason. Cast out, sit back, relax and wait for the fun to begin.

*Tracy Benton*
*Boca Raton, FL*

# Cheap and Very Effective Trout Bait

Place a small quantity of mini-marshmallows (white) in a plastic bag with a few drops of food coloring dye and shake around to coat. I have found yellow or orange to produce best. When fully coated, spread around on wax paper and sprinkle generous amount of powdered cheese (Parmesan or Romano) to coat fully and let dry. Garlic powder can also be used. These baits float off bottom—very effective. Fish these marshmellows as you would a Power Bait or other floating trout bait.

*Robert Kukuvka*
*Rockaway, NJ*

# Hooking Baitfish

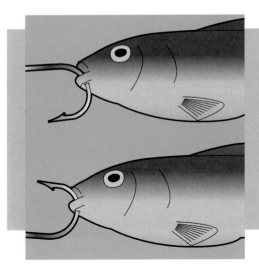

Whether we are a freshwater or saltwater angler, we all need (or like) to use minnows or other small baitfish. One of the best ways to catch a larger fish with the little shrimps is to hook them through the mouth. How you go about doing this is you hold the slimy thing in your hand quite securely and push the hook in at the base of the jaw and out through the typically open mouth.

*Tracy Benton*
*Boca Raton, FL*

## Slip Bobbers for Slip-Sinker Fishing

*How to tie a stop.*

Slip bobber stops are good for more than just slip bobbers. For anyone who ties their own slip bobber stops, I found a use for them besides slip-bobber fishing. I like to use them for slip sinker fishing plastic lizards in an adjustable Carolina rig or bottom fishing live bait. I found that using stops does not compromise the fishing line like smashing on a split-shot, or like using swivels where multiple knots must be trusted. I start with a slip sinker, a bead and two slip-bobber stops. Using two stops prevents the sinker from moving down the line during the cast. If you want a sinker to stay in one position, not sliding up or down, place a third knot and a second bead above the slip sinker. This method replaces the toothpick method, it may not be a faster method to rig up, but it will not pinch your line like a toothpick jammed into a slip sinker and it can be adjusted just as easily.

*Jim Whitenack
Muncie, IN*

# Fishing the Weeds

Weedy lakes are prime bobber-fishing targets. In most lakes, walleyes will use weed cover more than reefs, points or other classic bottom structure. Weeds provide an ideal habitat for walleyes. Ambush feeders by nature, walleyes lie in wait along weedlines or in dense stands of aquatic cover. When minnows or other tasty tidbits pass by, walleyes simply rush out and grab a quick meal.

Lakes with dense cabbage stands or other broad-leaf, submergent weed cover are difficult to fish with jigs, rigs or crankbaits.

A slip bobber is the ultimate vertical presentation for working weedlines or patches of thick aquatic vegetation. An electric motor and a pair of polarized fishing glasses are valuable aids for slip-bobbering the weeds.

An electric motor is ideal for quietly moving the boat while you're hunting for productive-looking weed edges or pockets. Polarized glasses make it easier to see submerged weedtops below the surface of the water.

When searching for weeds, get as high above the water's surface as you can. Stand on the casting deck, boat seat, cooler or anything that will give you a better vantage point. Once productive looking weeds are located, work the electric motor to properly position the boat.

You want your boat within an easy lob cast of the weeds. Lob casting the bobber rig is less likely to cause the minnow to be torn free during the cast, and the softer bobber landing is less likely to spook feeding fish.

Choose an opening in the weeds and flip the bobber rig into it. Start with the bait within 12 inches of the bottom; later, you may want to try suspending the bait farther off the bottom.

Resist the temptation to sit tight and wait for something to happen. The secret to fishing the weeds with slip bobbers is to keep moving until a group of fish is located. Cruise along silently with the electric motor and toss bobber rigs into other likely spots. If no bites occur within a couple of minutes, reel in, check the bait and make another cast. It's necessary to fish with fresh and lively bait at all times. A dead minnow or limp leech won't interest many walleyes.

Minnows usually are the best live bait for fishing weeds. Other species, including perch, bluegills and bullheads, also inhabit the weeds. Panfish will usually ignore a good-sized minnow, but a crawler or leech will attract every pesky panfish in the vicinity.

# Minnow Revival

Here is a good tip on how to revive minnows: Live bait left in a bait bucket will soon belly up and die. When this happens, drop 2 or 3 asprin tablets into the water. This will revive the bait and keep them lively for a few hours.

*Richard Johnson*
*Elida, OH*

# Elongated Leeches

To keep a leech from balling up, thread a short piece of surgical tubing over the shank of the hook. Hook the leech far enough back from the sucker so it can attach to the tubing. An "attached" leech is less likely to ball up.

*Kurt Beckstrom*
*Managing Editor, North American Fisherman*

# Quick Bait

After overnight rain, I harvest lots of nightcrawlers under boards left laying around on the ground (I put the boards on the ground for this purpose). The worms stay there right under the boards before going deeper underground.

*Stephen Turnis*
*Dubuque, IA*

# Successful Bait Transportation

My tip is for transporting alwives from one location to another to use as bait. In the past we would only have about fifty percent survive, so we bought a portable pump so we can keep the water circulating. This helps keep the fish fresh and we only end up losing one or two.

*Shawn Maloney*
*Enfield, CT*

# Cages for Crickets

Make your own cricket cages from plastic soft drink bottles. They have positive closures (screw lids) and they certainly are cheap. The green ones keep the critters calmer. Poke some holes in the bottle, or preferably burn them with a hot nail so the plastic doesn't crack.

*Richard Richter*
*Michigan City, IN*

# Trying Tadpoles

Few anglers use tadpoles as bait because they are delicate and often difficult to keep on the hook. Tadpoles do, however, attract all sorts of gamefish. If you keep casting to a minimum in order to reduce bait damage, it's possible to fish tadpoles. Put a sharp No. 8 wire Aberdeen hook gingerly through the tadpole's lips. When tadpoles are nearly mature, the hook can be inserted behind their developing legs. Hooks with wire ties also work. Tadpoles seem particularly good bait for big brown trout.

Tadpoles are most effective early in the summer when small frogs have just barely emerged from their tadpole waters. Many tadpole species have disappeared by midsummer. However, if you raise tadpoles in tanks and regulate the light duration or select bullfrog tadpoles that take longer to mature, you will be able to use these baits all year long.

# Trout Bait

Try this bait for trout: Mix garlic powder and Parmesan cheese with white miniature marshmallows. Store the mixture in an airtight container. This is good for both day and night fishing. If the marshmallows are not getting bites by themselves, try a nightcrawler or salmon eggs on the hook with them.

*John Medina*
*Canon City, CO*

# Bait for Crayfish

To get crayfish for bait, leave ground meat by the edge of the water at night. In the morning you will have more than enough crayfish to fish with.

*Jeff Swarthout*
*Barryton, MI*

# Keep Crayfish Alive

A friend and I were discussing how to keep a crayfish on a hook without puncturing its tail, which will ultimately kill it. So, what we came up with is this: Take your hook and lay it across the back of the crayfish. Then slide on a dental brace rubberband. Wrap the band around the crayfish body, including the hook shank. There you have it! He will now stay alive. You can double up with two or more rubberbands, depending on your preference. Good luck.

*Chris Thompson*
*Port Huron, MI*

# Easy Red Night Crawlers

If you want to color your night crawlers red, grind up some soft red brick and put it into your bedding box. In about 4 days the worms will absorb the color and turn a nice shade of red.

*Richard Johnson*
*Elida, OH*

# Float Tube Chumming

Sometimes when I fish from my float tube, I'll hang a chum bucket (a small can with dog or cat food inside, and holes punched in the can to allow food to disperse) off the side of the tube. Before long, minnows will congregate around the can. This in turn, attracts larger fish to the tube. I then vertical jig with small crappie jigs or minnow jigs. This method is deadly and has never failed me.

*Kong Shang*
*Reno, NV*

***Editor's note: Check with your state's regulations to see if chumming is legal in your state.

# Color Makes a Difference

Use redworms for bait, rather than regular gray earthworms. This has been tried in a wading pool with a warmouth, who would zip across the pool to nail a redworm, but would ignore a gray one right in front of his nose. It's presumably the red color that does the trick.

*Richard Richter*
*Michigan City, IN*

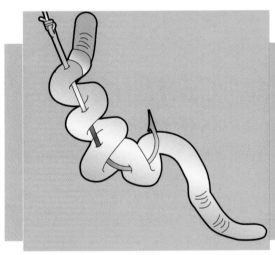

# Worm Presentation

We all know that fish love earthworms, but to make those wrigglers look better, my family has a special secret. I will share it with you here. First, you grab a worm. The fatter and longer, the better. The first place you put the hook through is right behind the broad band where the worm's hearts are. Then, wrap it around the hook once and put that next part in. Repeat this a few times, leaving about 1-inch dangling off.

*Tracy Benton*
*Boca Raton, FL*

# Catch Your Own Crawdads

If you want to catch crayfish for bait, use an ordinary wire-mesh minnow trap. Enlarge the openings to catch larger crayfish. Bait the trap with a perforated can of cat food made from fish by-products, or a container of bacon grease.

*Dan Carlson*
*Two Harbors, MN*

# Chumming with Soft Panfish Baits

**B**luegills and crappie love live bait, but I prefer Berkley Crappie Nuggets or other soft panfish baits that mold to the hook. The reason is simple: As you start hooking panfish, the soft bait disintegrates and spreads through the water. It creates a chumming effect that not only draws panfish in from a distance, but triggers a feeding frenzy that maggots or minnows simply cannot duplicate.

*Jonathan Storm*
*Senior Editor, North American Fisherman*

# Keep Those Worms Cool

**I**f you're a fisherman that likes to fish the entire day, but can't seem to keep your bait fresh and alive, especially on those hot summer days, then this may be what you need. Try using one of those small coolers that are about the size of a six-pack of soda. You can usually find one at a discount store for about $5.00. Then just put some dirt and worm food in it, along with your worms, and store it in the refrigerator. On your next big day of fishing, you'll have fresh worms the entire day. And on those really hot days, use a small reusable ice pack in the cooler for added protection.

*James Pratt*
*Clayton, IL*

# Keep Your Baits Alive Longer

**A** way to keep baitfish or shrimp alive longer is to keep the water shallow in a wide bucket. If at all possible, put a few plants in the bucket, both for a place to hide and for oxygen. Try to scare the bait as little as possible when grabbing some.

*Tracy Benton*
*Boca Raton, FL*

# Live Bait Storage

**I**f you have two live wells in your boat (one for fish and one for baitfish) put two bags of unopened ice in the smaller of the two instead of filling it with water. That way you can put a variety of bait and food in the same place.

*Travis Pond*
*Grand Blanc, MI*

# Catfish Bait Keepers

**T**o keep delicate catfish baits such as chicken livers or putrefied fish from coming apart in the water, wrap them in a mesh bag made from a piece of cheesecloth, orange sack or a nylon stocking. This prevents your bait from washing away, and the catfish don't seem to notice the difference.

*Keith Sinders*
*Brazil, IN*

# Sure-Fire Catfish Rig

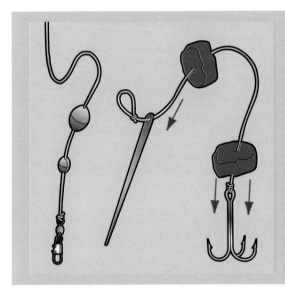

**R**un your line through an egg sinker (or sinker of choice) and bead-tie on a snap swivel of your size choice. I tie a treble hook (it doesn't have to be huge) on an 18 inch or longer mono leader and tie a loop on the other end. Use a large plastic or steel needle (from a dime store, dollar store or department store). Thread your leader loop through the needle eye—push the needle through your bait—pull the leader through and snug the bait onto the treble. This will act as a cradle under your bait and will hold it firm. Thus allowing strong, long casts and will hold firm in even heavy current. Tie up and bait several rigs when you are fishing. Then all that is required for fast re-baiting is to unsnap and snap on another pre-baited leader/hook. Let the extra baits set in the sun to toughen and ripen up.

*Jack Linder*
*Kirbyville, MO*

# Improvise Bait

**I**n case you have a desire to wet a line and haven't had the opportunity to prepare, keep some bait with you at all times. Get some of the dog food that looks like marrow bones. Take out the marrow and keep it in a small plastic bag to keep it moist. It works fine for bluegills and stays on the hook fairly well.

*Richard Richter*
*Michigan City, IN*

# Manageable Live Bait Leader

**M**any walleye anglers are going to leaders as long as 12 feet when live bait rigging. These leaders may help increase bite numbers, but they make landing a fish difficult. The solution: add an adjustable bobber stop above your swivel, but below your sinker. Tighten tag ends of stop enough to hold the sinker in place, but keep it loose enough that you can reel the sinker down to the swivel when fighting a fish. It may take a bit of experimentation to get it right. Leave the tag ends long.

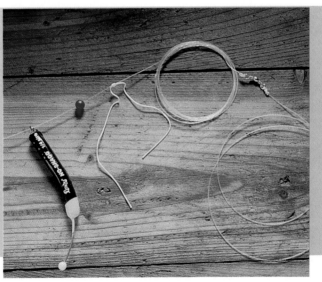

*Steve Pennaz*
*Executive Director, North American Fisherman*

# Care and Handling of Bait Worms

**W**orms kept cool and damp can survive 2 or 3 months in a commercial bedding material or a homemade mix of half shredded newspaper and half leaf mold. If worms dry out, they will die. Therefore, if you're buying worms from a commercial outlet, you should always check their quality. Worms from local bait shops or the ubiquitous rural worm magnate operating behind a "Worms For Sale" sign normally are in better shape than those purchased from a retail chain outlet.

If you can, choose the lively worms over the couch potatoes. Rinse the worms, if possible, so you can better see that they are in good condition. (This also saves time on the water because you won't have to grade worms when you should be fishing.) Most quality worm outlets sell well-conditioned worms that are fatter and larger than average. You can also condition worms yourself in a day or so. What's most important is that their texture is firm and, of course, that they are the proper size for the fish you're seeking. Generally, you can improve worm texture by storing them for several weeks in damp—not sopping wet—sand.

Whether you buy or glean worms, investing in worm containers makes sense. Commercial cardboard containers are okay for a short time period. Lay some strips of wet paper on top of the worms, then put some weight on the top. The worms will absorb the water and expand in size.

Many expert anglers use two containers. A basic, insulated container, like a commercial worm box or a homemade Styrofoam box, works well. During hot weather, insert either a plastic container of ice or a refreezable pack so worms neither drown in excess water from the ice melt nor cook in the sun. You should place the worm container on a cushion or pad in your car or pickup when driving to the water; excess vibrations can kill worms.

Ready containers need not be fancy. Tin cans work, but they are easier to use if a wire is attached in holes punched near the top of the can. A tobacco tin also works nicely if you punch air holes in the cover. Such tins also slide easily into a pocket or vest for carrying when your hands are full of gear. On very hot days, place a well-rinsed, soaked kitchen sponge in the container lid. A flip-flop, metal, belt-mounted bait container works exceptionally well as a ready box for stream fishermen. It can be restocked with a dozen or more worms as needed. Damp sphagnum moss works nicely in such containers and wet, shredded newspaper works in a pinch. The moss has the added benefit of improving the worms texture; it tends to scour out any ingested dirt. As a result, the worms are tougher and more lively, too.

Another effective way to tote worms is in corrugated cardboard rolls. Tear the smooth, outer layer off one side of a 5- by 15-inch piece of corrugated cardboard and place a few worms on the cardboard. Most will slide immediately into the slots while the others can be pushed in. Moisten the cardboard slightly and roll it up; store the rolled cardboard in a sealable plastic bag or a tin container with a lid. Worms will remain happy all day. As you need bait, simply unroll the cardboard. A few pieces of cardboard in the traditional flip-top tobacco can works, too.

Presorting worms by size saves time on the water. To customize your bait to your hook size, it's worthwhile to sort your bait into several ready containers. Tote a container of 2- to 3-inch worms for stream trout or bluegills, another for 4- or 5-inch worms for crappies and a third with your biggest nightcrawlers for larger gamefish.

A worm's color seems to make a difference in some water conditions. In clear water, for example, the choice seems to be very well-conditioned, almost translucent worms. If some purists are correct, fish can distinguish among colors, so you might want to produce your own "technicolor" worms. Adding brick dust to the worms' storage bed creates "really red" worms. For other colors, saturate your storage container with various vegetable dyes.

Many anglers believe such bright-colored worms can help in clear water. Even with a light bobber rig, you'll see some bites only when the bright worm disappears as it's nipped by a fish. Following drifts when freelining worms is much easier if a bright-colored worm is used, too.

Whether the worms were gleaned and raised or purchased in bulk and saved until needed, large containers filled with commercial worm bedding or a homemade mix of good loose soil and leaf mold enable you to keep worms for months. A worm pit can be as simple as a box or frame lined with mesh or wood set into soft ground in a shady spot. Replace the soil once a year. A lid conserves moisture and keeps active worms, like African nightcrawlers in, and local animals and birds out.

In areas subject to frozen ground or rocky or clay soil, consider using above-ground containers, such as half-wine barrels or boxes. Almost anything works as a container, although metal containers should be painted inside and out so they won't rust out. Don't forget to provide screened drainage holes in the bottom of your worm farm so the worms don't drown! Be sure metal and other above-ground boxes are protected from direct sunlight and from freezing. Straw mulch also helps protect worms in below-ground boxes that are subject to frigid temperatures.

Fill the box with commercial worm mix or simply layer in sod or leaf mold with friable (crumbled) soil. Wait long enough to ensure the worm bedding doesn't compost and warm the material past 50 degrees, causing them to die. Then, add about 50 nightcrawlers or 150 earthworms per cubic foot. The next day remove any dead or dying worms and chop, freeze and use them for chum. Keep the growth container moist, but not wet.

It takes about two months for worms to reproduce and four to six months for their offspring to reach full-size. With good management, each cubic foot of soil will produce 1,000 to 2,000 redworms and 300 to 500 nightcrawlers a year.

Feeding the worms isn't difficult. Every two months blend a mix of ½ cup lard and 2 cups cornmeal into the top 2 inches of dirt. It's easy to see the yellow meal; when the yellow disappears, it's time to feed again. Some worm growers use a split grapefruit, placing it cut-side down on top of the worm bedding. When the soft pulp disappears, it's time for more. Use caution when feeding; overfeeding kills more worms than underfeeding.

Desperate anglers who have run out of their worm supplies when the first spring rains are coloring the waters and the fish are gobbling worms can often find worms near streams, around dead and decaying wood and under stumps. Carry a few sealable plastic bags to hold such baits of opportunity. Having a trowel or shovel handy sure helps. Digging worms on the stream bank itself is not beneficial to the riparian habitat or the stream's water quality. It's not recommended.

# *4* STORAGE

**A**nglers have a lot of "stuff." There's just no getting around it. If you had one rod, one reel, one package of hooks or one lure … you wouldn't be into fish very often because you wouldn't be at all versatile. So we need our stuff. All of it. But we're always needing more and more ideas on how to store and organize it all so it's at our fingertips, ready for action. Here's how NAFC members are storing and organizing their stuff … ideas for how you can do it even better.

## Measure This

Never, ever be without a measuring stick. I mark my rod from the butt to the 36-inch mark at 3-inch intervals with waterproof tape. I like the thin, white tape used in first aid kits. It's made to stick to questionable surfaces (skin is always oily) and it's easy to write on.

*Edward Pace*
*Factoryville, PA*

## Split-Shot Solution

Here's a handy way to store your split-shot sinkers when not in use. Put them in empty Tic-Tac dispensers for an easy to use, one-at-a-time release. You'll never have to fumble around in a tiny bag or spin the plastic wheels on a circular sinker container again.

*Terry Sires*
*Chandler, OK*

## Just What the Doctor Ordered

An excellent storage container for your flies could be only as far away as your medicine cabinet. Empty prescription bottles are great for this job. They are waterproof and inexpensive. Also, their childproof lids insure no unwanted openings of the bottle. Just fill the bottles up and mark the lids so you know what is in the bottle.

*Mitchell Masuda*
*Salinas, CA*

## Terminal Tackle Storage

Old 35 millimeter film containers make very handy containers for terminal tackle such as hooks, jigs, swivels, sinkers and the like. I use several multi-compartment tackle boxes. In each compartment I place one or several film containers filled with various terminal tackle. On the side and top of each film container I place a sticker with the contents labeled. This keeps terminal tackle organized and readily available.

*Joseph Islinger*
*Des Plaines, IL*

# Tackle Organizer

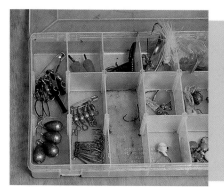

**S**tore small pieces of tackle "loose" in the trays in your tackle box and you'll eventually find yourself with quite a mess. To keep it all straight, slide snaps, swivels, split rings and bell sinkers onto safety pins for safe keeping. Other small items such as hooks and split-shot can be kept in aspirin bottles.

*Adam Doran*
*Ames, IA*

# Storing Soft-Plastics

**H**ere is a fast, easy, money-saving way to store your Berkley soft-plastic baits. Put them in a hard plastic, 3-ring binder. Poke 1 or 2 holes in the bag depending on the size of it, then you stick the bag in the rings of the binder. You can buy these binders at almost any store for less than one dollar.

*Jamie McGuire*
*Glastonbury, CT*

# Use Film Containers for Tackle

**T**his is a tip that everyone should know. Use old film canisters to keep snap swivels and other small fishing tackle in (it also keeps them dry). I also use film containers to keep pork rinds inside (they don't rust and discolor inside the plastic).

*John C. Gallo*
*Uniondale, NY*

# Handy Hook Container

**H**ot glue a magnet to the inside of an empty 35 millimeter film container lid. The empty film container makes a handy hook storage box and the magnet will always provide you with an untangled hook ready to use.

*Matthew Radzialowski*
*Wixom, MI*

# Store It

**M**any states give a free plastic license holder to anglers. Collect such holders and use them to house small, needed items like leads, hooks, short pieces of monofilament ... and of course your licenses or permits.

*Ed O'Connor*
*Hanson, MA*

# Hook Storage

**A**re you getting tired of small fish hooks falling in your tackle box and when you go to reach them they stick your fingers? I have a simple solution. Keep a small magnet in your tackle box!

*Sam Wyatt*
*Owensboro, KY*

# Avoid Tackle Box Tangles

**I**nstead of having a bunch of loose hooks lying around in your tackle box or getting tangled together in the boxes, just glue a strip of Styrofoam or a sponge to the side of the tackle box and hang the hooks on that.

*Lee Jones*
*Davie, FL*

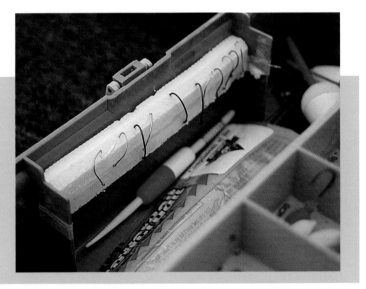

# World's Smallest Tackle Box

**O**ld, plastic snuff cans make good tackle boxes for sinkers, hooks and plastic baits. These containers are small, convenient, durable, worm-proof and fit into your pocket. Not to mention the price is right!

*Coleby Gilliand*
*Deatsville, AL*

# Take Care of Your Spinnerbait Skirts

**H**ere's a hint to keep spinnerbait skirts from sticking together or drying out when not in use: After a spinnerbait or any bait with a rubber or vinyl skirt has been used, shake the water out of the spinnerbait and place the bait in a Ziploc bag with 2 tablespoons of talcum powder. The next time the spinnerbait will be used, the skirt will be dry and pliable and ready for use. No sticking together or curling up.

*Andy Krotje*
*Fair Lawn, NJ*

# Secure the Snells

I have found an effective method for storing worm harnesses, floating worm rigs and other pre-rigs with a length of snelled line attached, after they have been used and removed from their original packaging. I use very small Ziplock plastic bags (such as the kind that lead split-shot is sold in). I cut a piece of cardboard small enough to just fit inside the Ziplock bag. I cut a notch at each corner of the cardboard. Beginning with the looped end of the snelled line, I wrap the snell, then the rig, around the edge of the cardboard, passing the line through each notch in the cardboard. The last step is to secure the hook and place the cardboard in the Ziplock bag. I use a lot of these rigs, so I have an old zippered bag which I put a couple dozen of these rigs into. They never tangle, can be readily seen through the clear plastic, and are ready to use when needed.

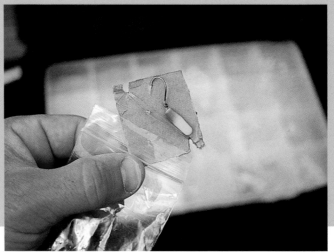

*Joseph H. Islinger*
*Des Plaines, IL*

# Storage Idea

My storage idea is to use film containers to hold different items. I take first aid tape and wrap it around the container and through a key ring. Depending on the size of the ring used, I can either hook it on a clip on my tackle box or vest. On my boat I use a similar method, only with Velcro tape attached to the container and pieces of Velcro attached to strategic places. I like to use a Sharpie permanent marker to write the container's contents on the cover. These work well for all the little things you seem to have around while fishing.

*Tom Pimental*
*Whitman, MA*

# Tackle Storage Tip

No room in your tackle box for big baits? Then try this trick. Hang your lures around the rim of a foam minnow bucket or cooler. The lures won't get tangled up and you'll be able to easily find the bait you're looking for.

*F.W. Walker*
*Barrie, Ontario, Canada*

# Tangle Free Storage

I use those small plastic tubes and resealable plastic bags (that you get with things like small gypsie jigs or flies and curly tails or sassy shad) to double up small terminal tackle like sinkers and swivels. I use the bags for walleye snells or crankbaits. Also, when I get Rapalas, I keep them in the boxes to put another box-less one with it.

*Travis Pond*
*Grand Blanc, MI*

# Close-to-Home Action

Live bait—where it's not prohibited—can take a variety of gamefish right around home. You should invest in a 5-foot ultra-light rig and some terminal tackle and let neighborhood panfish challenge your skills. For children, rig a simple cane pole with a bobber, small hook and a lively worm—you've eliminated a lot of tackle hassle. Fishing with live bait can be simple and inexpensive because terminal tackle costs are small. You can save even more if you make your own bobbers, cast your own weights and wrap your own rods. Bait fishing is great sport; it can be one of the most complex forms of fishing in freshwater!

Over 1,000 different live baits are possible if you add up the many species of minnows, baitfish, worms, leeches, frogs, toads, salamanders, crayfish, shrimp, aquatic insects, terrestrial insects and larvae. Compound this with double rigs—where legal—that let you offer two or more baits at a time. Consider the multitude of hook choices to match the variety of live bait sizes and types, the addition of dead or preserved baits and the host of bobbers designed for different techniques in still and moving waters.

Compound the many bobbers, sinkers and lure/bait combinations possible and it's clear that mastery of live-bait fishing in all of its complexity is as likely as winning a lottery. Fortunately, one need not master everything about bait fishing to catch fish the first time out. It's comforting, however, to know that the challenge exists.

# Keys to Finding Great Lake Perch

**G**reg wilkins, a Lake Michigan enigma, maintains that even though northern Lake Michigan now holds a bountiful supply of jumbo yellow perch, it isn't always easy to catch them. The way to a cooler full of perch is to first find them.

"If you can find 'em, you can catch 'em," Wilkins said. "Perch are nomadic gamefish to a certain extent. Granted, they don't wander all over the lake like a school of coho salmon, but perch do move around as they search for food."

The eastern shoreline of Lake Michigan, and particularly the 120 miles of shoreline from Ludington north to Leland (which includes Platte Bay where Wilkins often fishes), is now home to some of North America's finest yellow perch fishing. The perch are present, but the day-to-day problem is locating the schools of fish, and it can be difficult.

"A small Loran-C is used to facilitate finding my favorite rock piles," Wilkins said. "I've committed most of the submerged rock piles to memory by triangulating their location with objects on shore, but by punching in the coordinates on my Loran-C, it's a simple matter to leave the rivermouth and be anchored over the rocks in a matter of 2 or 3 minutes.

He believes the one big secret to consistent jumbo yellow perch catches is learning the exact location of these major fish factories. Perch frequent the reefs and rock piles for just one reason—to feed on the abundant forage base.

Rocks and submerged reefs are usually situated along major drop-offs near deep water, and the water depth over this underwater structure will range from 12 to 22 feet in most areas. The rocks—usually large boulders—occurred either naturally or were placed in these locations during dredge-and-fill operations off large rivermouth areas when the U.S. Army Corps of Engineers constructed breakwalls, piers or harbors of refuge many years ago.

"The placement of these rocks on the lake bottom has been a real lifesaver for perch fishermen," Wilkins noted. "The submerged rocks and reefs attract emerald shiners, alewife fry and crayfish, and this forage base attracts and holds yellow perch."

Wilkins noted that although the locations of these forage-producing rocks may be well-known to local anglers, they can be difficult to find for fishermen new to the area. But, he said, perch fishermen are gregarious, and usually are willing to let newcomers anchor nearby once they locate a school of active fish.

"Finding the fish means more than just knowing where the rock piles are located," Wilkins said. A fisherman must know how large the underwater rock formations are. They must also know where nearby muck beds are found because the perch will feed on the larval insects emerging from the mud. Anglers need to be able to experimentally fish several areas over the rocks or near the muck beds until they find schools of fish.

"Perch may frequent a specific rock pile for days on end," Wilkins said. "Then, for no apparent reason, the fish may move 20 yards, or as much as two miles, to feed over another similar underwater structure. Consistently catching these fish means knowing where 2 or 3 reefs or rock piles are located, and then fishing near bottom in several locations over each one until the fish are found."

Wilkins relies both on his Loran-C and an electronic flasher to pinpoint schools of fish under the boat. The Loran-C gets him to the underwater structure and the flasher allows him to detect the presence or absence of fish.

# 5
## Chapter Five
# BOATS

A boat is a beautiful thing — taking you to your fishing grounds, providing the vessel in which you create many happy memories. But a boat is also a lot of work. It seems there's never an end to the maintenance and tuning you can be doing. And that's okay, a part of the game. But there are ways to make the work a little easier, so you can get more enjoyment and fishing time out of your rig. NAFC members share their insights and ideas on the upcoming pages.

# Don't Lose Those Plates

I had both bolts fall off of my license plate on my boat trailer at different times. The second time I didn't have access to a spare bolt, so I improvised with a large split ring that I took from a bottle opener. Now it will never come off and I won't worry about losing my license plate.

*Mike Carns*
*Henderson, NV*

# Push Pole Fishing

When you fish out on the flats and use a push pole instead of a motor, tie a piece of rope to the end of the pole. Then take the other end and tie it to your boat so that if the pole slips out of your hands you will always be able to retrieve it.

*Sean Merritt*
*Sugar Land, TX*

# Secure the Gear

Tired of your anchor, tackle and gear bouncing and slamming around below deck on your boat? Whether trailering your boat down the highway or running 50 mph plus to that secret fishing hole, everything stored below deck wants to move. One sure solution to help hold things in place is to line your boat's lockers with plastic outdoor carpeting. You know, the carpet that looks like green plastic grass. Used carpet works just as well. The outdoor carpet will cut down on things moving and breaking.

*Captain Del Dykes*
*Kailua-Kona, HI*

# Secure Your Motor

If you have trouble with your electric motor slipping on your transom, go to your auto parts store and get two freeze plugs the size of your motor screw plates.

*Claude Andrews*
*Richmond, VA*

# A Different Kind of Texas Rigging

During a recent fishing trip to a lake in Texarkana, Texas, I had a little problem. As I was crossing the lake to my favorite fishing hole, I noticed that water was rapidly coming into my boat. I immediately headed for shore, but was eventually forced to swim beside the boat when it became too full. On shore, I drained the boat and began to search for the problem. I thought I had left the plug out, but instead found a hole about the size of a marble in the bottom. Searching for a patch, I took some plastic worms and stuffed the leak temporarily. But the worms kept falling out. So I used a cigarette lighter to melt them. The resulting "goo" plugged the hole long enough for me to get back to the boat ramp. I know this is not something one would do for a permanent repair, but I now keep a cigarette lighter in my tackle box all the time because it was a lifesaver that day.

*Curtis Clifton*
*Texarkana, TX*

## One Man Boat Loader

I used to have trouble loading and unloading my boat by myself. So I took a wheel from an old shopping cart (the wheel that has the bolt on it) and drilled a hole in the front of my boat. Then I attached the wheel from the shopping cart. Now when I get home, I just push the boat along on the wheel and I don't have to wait for anyone to help me. When I go fishing, the boat just rolls away from the car wonderfully.

*Albert Rodzinak*
*Middlesex, NJ*

## Bug-Free Storage

When storing your boat or camper for any length of time, purchase a large citronella candle, remove the lid and place it (unlit, of course) inside the camper/boat. This will keep all the creepy-crawly things out. Larger campers may require several more to properly disperse the bugs and the scent will not linger long after the candles are removed.

*William Cooley*
*Bonnots Mill, MO*

## Don't Scratch Your Boat

When you replace the boat numbers and letters, don't try to scrape them off or you will scratch up the boat. Simply heat them with a hair dryer until they get soft enough for you to pull off.

*Steve VonBrandt*
*Wilmington, DE*

## Speed Control Means More Fish

When fishing shallow water or spooky fish, I've found that keeping my bow-mounted electric motor at a low, but steady speed is better than using bursts of higher power. Fish tolerate constant noises, but shy away from loud, irregular noises.

*Steve Pennaz*
*Executive Director, North American Fisherman*

## Remove Milfoil Buildup

Now that milfoil is everywhere, more fisherman are getting weeds caught in the prop. A simple tip is to lock down the tilt release and from a standstill put the outboard into reverse. Increase the throttle at a rapid rate in several short bursts. This should clear the weeds off your prop in a hurry.

*Terry Brodsky*
*Minnetonka, MN*

# Longwall Tactics

**D**ams spanning a wide chasm between hills or mountains usually have a long, concrete wall (called the "longwall") filling the large expanse. If a hydroelectric station is built into the dam, it will usually be at one end of the dam; and, most of the released water will flow through its turbines. By comparison, dams without turbine generation release water through a tunnel-like spillway often at one end of the dam.

The longwall normally has a series of floodgates on top that can be opened to increase water flow during a potential flood situation. To break up the overflow from the floodgates, large rocks and boulders are often piled into a wedge or flat, just downstream from the longwall. They reduce the current's force just like the alligator claws do in a turbine discharge area. Ultimately, a deep ditch develops between the longwall and this current break—a canal that holds catfish.

That current break's shallow lip often serves as a hotspot for catfish anglers. While the deepest portion of the ditch or canal acts as a sanctuary, the shallower areas are a quick, convenient feeding ground. Cats will roam the entire rocky structure, but activity seems to center around that slope from shallow to deep water. And, don't overlook the deep-water sanctuary for success.

Because these areas are rather large and removed from the direct current flow, they cannot be fished very well by using a current drift. Instead, anchor over the top of the lip and cast a few bottom rigs around the boat. If you prefer remaining on the move, try drifting with the wind or easing around with the trolling motor while bouncing a bait off the bottom directly under the boat. These current breaks can be particularly rough on your terminal tackle. Bouncing your bait vertically under the boat can minimize snags, tackle loss and conserve fishing time.

Catfish often spawn in the rocky crevices of current breaks that are within 4 to 6 feet of the surface. While there is no hard, firm evidence supporting that fact, it does make sense. For whatever reason, catfish are found in these rocky areas during the spawning season, often pouncing on bait bounced off the bottom. If you think cats may be spawning there, try this: Slip a piece of cut bait onto a 1-ounce, leadhead jig and probe the bottom with it. The round, heavy jig rolls off the rocks and into the holes underneath. If a nesting cat is there, it will smash the bait. It will hit it hard and fast. Try pulling the fish out of its subterranean lair as quickly as possible. Obviously, you should use heavy lines and stout tackle.

# Clean Up Your Battery

**I**f you want to clean your trolling motor battery posts, set your battery out in a heavy rain. It will make those posts look like new.

*Bill Stalego*
*Newark, OH*

# Back the Boat Up

If you have problems backing your boat into the garage, try marking the exact spot where the boat should stop. First, position the trailer where you want it, then outline one of the tires with chalk. Next, pull the boat ahead and paint the chalk outline with bright, household paint. Now you'll know exactly where to position the boat the first time, every time—just back up until the trailer tire rests in the painted box.

Nick Farafontoff
El Dorado Hills, CA

# Mouse Proof Your Motor

If you must store your outboard motor in a shed, put a glue-board mouse trap inside the engine cowling. As an added precaution, pull the choke handle all the way out to keep the mice out of your carburetor. This will help prevent any unpleasant discoveries when you take the boat out next spring.

Brice Umstead
Knoxville, TN

# Quiet Please

An inexpensive way to cut noise in an aluminum johnboat or canoe is to line the top of the gunwales with foam pipe wrap. It's available pre-cut, in different sizes; just slide it over the rails to prevent the smacking of rods against the boat. The foam doubles as an excellent place to hang jig heads, spinnerbaits, crankbaits or anything with a hook.

Wayne Loudermilk
Charlottesville, VA

# Protect Your Boat Cover

To make your boat cover last longer, protect it from wear at the windshield area by splitting a piece of hose and slipping it over the windshield before covering the boat. Use a piece of garden hose or clear soft plastic hose available at a hardware store. This protects the cover from the sharp edges. Cut additional pieces of hose and place on the gunwales of your aluminum johnboat or V-bottom boat ... it protects rods and quiets the boat if your fishing rod knocks up against the side of the boat.

Homer Lee
East Stroudsburg, PA

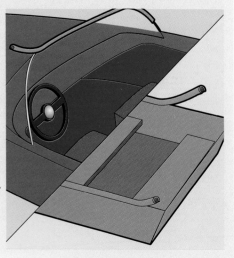

# Boats and Motors

I have found a way to keep mice out of your motor when you store it away. I've learned that if you pull the choke and leave it like that until you bring it back out, mice will not be able to enter your motor.

Michael Thomas Bryan
Pollocksville, NC

# 6 RODS & REELS

**W**hat an investment a good rod-and-reel combo can be these days! Who would have dreamt it when you were growing up, riding your bike down to the creek with your Zebco 33 and fiberglass rod, or walking down to the pond with a canepole and can of worms? It pays to take good care of the expensive equipment you've graduated to, and to know how to get the most out of it. Here's what NAFC members had to say about these matters.

# Natural Ferrule Lubrication

Whenever I put a fishing rod together, whether it be a freshwater rod or a saltwater rod, I carefully rub the ferrules on my face where my nose joins the rest of my face. This gives the ferrules a light coating of human oil and prevents the ferrules from sticking when I disassemble my rod.

*Richard Johnson*
*Elida, OH*

# Don't Lose Parts

When taking your fishing reel apart for cleaning, use an old egg carton to put the parts in. Number each compartment of the carton. Take your reel apart and place parts in numbered compartments. Reverse when putting back together. No misplaced or lost parts.

*David Behling*
*Little Chute, WI*

# Reviving Reels

How many of us come across an old gummed-up reel that won't even come apart? First, spray the reel inside and out with WD-40 (I like Slick 50). Wrap the reel in paper towels—make sure it's completely covered—wrap rubber bands around it. Drop it into a Ziplock bag. Seal the top and allow it to sit in a cool, dry place for two weeks (tops).

*Paul Winstead, Jr.*
*Mount Vernon, OH*

# Wax Your Rods

To keep my rods lasting longer and keep a lot of build-up off, I use some car wax to wax my rods. After a day of fishing, I just hose off the rods and they are clean. Nothing stays stuck on the rods.

*John C. Gallo*
*Uniondale, NY*

# Rod Travel Case

This is a money-saving tip that will help members who are going to travel and want to take their favorite rod. Go to your local hardware store on 'stocking day' and ask if they have any cardboard tubes. Normally they throw them out so you should get them for free. Cut it down to what ever size will fit your rod the best. I hope this tip helps. Good fishing!

*Paul Mulvin*
*Erie, PA*

# Custom Line Stripper

When it's time to change line on your favorite reel, stripping line becomes an easy task with your own custom line stripper used with any 3/8-inch electric drill. Simply take an empty plastic line spool and cut the arbor in half with a hacksaw. Use a 3/8-inch carriage bolt about 3/12-inch longer than the length of the spool together with a 3/8-inch washer and wing nut. The end of the bolt fits nicely into the drill chuck and the spool can be opened easily to discard the unwanted line afterwards. You'll be amazed at how quickly and neatly your custom line stripper works. Chances are your fishing buddies will want one too.

*Captain Del Dykes*
*Kailua-Kona, HI*

# Backlash Fix

Here's quick backlash trick. If your baitcaster backlashes, push hard on the spool with your left thumb while cranking 4 to 5 times with your right. This allows you to easily pull out light to moderate backlashes about 80 percent of the time.

*Kurt Beckstrom*
*Managing Editor, North*
*American Fisherman*

## The Terminal Test

In selecting the right rod, the first thing to check is the weight it tosses best, and how that relates to the total weight of the terminal tackle you'll be using. Other things being equal, lighter is better. Look for the lightest rod that will cover your needs. For example, if you fish unweighted worms in moving water, a small ultra-light rod rated for 1/8- to 1/2-ounce terminal tackle and bait could be the best choice. If you will be casting massive suckers for pike, a rod rated for 2, 3 or more ounces will work best.

Although these ratings relate to line test, there is a proportional relationship between terminal tackle weight and line test which varies from rod to rod. These ratings can be useful in matching your needs.

# Wax Your Reels

Apply auto wax to the inside bell housing of spincast reels for increased casting distance.

*Robert Kukuvka*
*Rockaway, NJ*

# Spool Protection

While I use different pound test line on a number of spare reels, I found to keep the line from coming off, I use Velcro straps cut to size and place them around the spool.

*John C. Gallo*
*Uniondale, NY*

# Secure Rods

To keep your rods from getting all wound up from either bouncing around in the vehicle or just sitting at home, first hook the lure to your reel. Then tighten the line up, pull the line away from the pole and wrap it around the pole so the guideline on the pole will catch it. This prevents dangling and loose lines.

*Kyle Gauderman*
*Glenfield, ND*

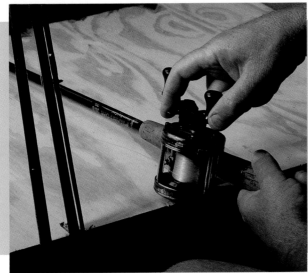

# Don't Leave Your Star Drag Locked Down

**I**f you are putting your fishing gear in storage until next season or for an unknown amount of time, loosen your star drag before tucking your reel away. Spring washers are usually installed in the drag system and leaving them compressed for a long time can reduce the span of your drag.

*William L. McCabe*
*Napa, CA*

# Neat Tricks for Protecting Rods

**H**ere's a useful tip for members who regularly carry their rods in the back of a pickup or similar vehicle. Instead of a rod case, I use an old rifle or shotgun case. They will handle all but the longest 2-piece rods, and you can leave the reels attached. Each case can hold two rods.

*James Carucio*
*Marengo, IL*

# Packing Tackle

**T**his is an idea my son came up with. For kids that walk to the lake to fish, they can carry their rod and tackle box by putting the tackle box in the backpack and closing it then putting the rod through the straps with the reel in the middle (if same backpack design). You can also carry an empty live bait container by putting it inside the straps.

*John Pugel*
*West Allis, WI*

# Use Ponytail Holders for Rod Storage

**W**hen I take my rods apart, I use ponytail holders to keep them tightly together for storage. You also can identify your rods by the different colors when in a trunk of a car with other rods similar to yours. Ponytail holders come in a multitude of colors.

*William Biacco*
*Oakdale, PA*

# Rod Wrap

**W**hen transporting rods already rigged up with lures, I have found a cheap and quick method to protect exposed hooks. I use 3 to 4 wraps of common plastic cling wrap around the lure.

*Robert Kukuvka*
*Rockaway, NJ*

# Set Your Bait Fishing Rod on Automatic

When bait fishing, you can miss the bite if you aren't paying close attention. The fish can take the bait, feel the line and drop your bait. Use a sliding sinker and set your rod on "automatic". To set your rod up this way, put a rubberband on the rod above your reel. The rubberband should be snug around the rod. Make your cast and mend your slack line. Take a small loop of line between your first eye and the reel, then put it under the rubberband. You can adjust the amount of pull it takes to free the line by the amount of line under the rubberband. Open your bail (spinning reel) or unlock your spool (casting reel). When the fish takes the bait, the small loop will pull free leaving your reel on free spool. Adjust the spool tension on your casting reel to avoid backlash. The fish won't detect anything until you close the bail or lock your spool and are ready to set the hook.

*William L. McCabe*
*Napa, CA*

# Simple Rod Hanger

Here's how to make a simple but effective storage system for your fishing rods. Fasten three eye screws to the ceiling of your basement, garage or shed. Attach a short length of string through the eye of the first screw so it forms a loop large enough to hold the rod handle. Do the same for the other two screws. Just slide your rod through the loops so one supports the tip and another supports the mid-section and finally the handle.

*Collin Riley*
*Arlington, VA*

# Efficient Line Removal

To remove old line from your reel, use a power drill. Put an old supply spool or some large-capacity object in the drill bit head, tie the line to it and run the drill until the line is off your reel.

*Ollie Wiitala*
*Dexter, MI*

# Traveling Idea

I'd like to share an idea that has worked out well for me. I travel extensively and always take a number of fishing rods with me. Unfortunately, my large rod case doesn't fit into the compact rental cars that I drive. I solved the problem with two 1-foot sections of PVC pipe, four suction cups, two short bungee cords and a short length of rope. Attach one suction cup toward each end of the 1-foot sections of PVC pipe. Stick the suction cup/PVC combinations to the trunk of the car. Lay your rod case on top of the suction cup/PVC structure and bungee the rod case on securely. A rope tied to the front bumper and two around the middle keep the case from blowing off.

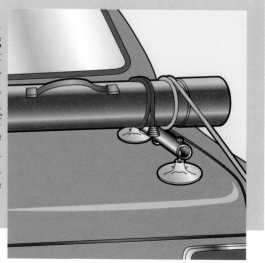

*Lester Kuhn*
*Derby, NY*

# Secure Storage

When the fishing trip is over and it's time to put the rods away, I like to secure my rods with ties. You know those little wire ties that come in boxes of trash bags? They make perfect ties for your fishing poles. A lot of people break down their poles for storage. The pole breaks down into two parts. They are usually held together by the natural snugness of the fishing line when it is reeled up tight and some line is wrapped around the handle and secured with the hook being stuck in the handle (if it's made of cork) or hooked on the reel handle. When you take the pole out of storage, the line has usually come loose and you have a tangled mess. I use the ties from garbage bags to secure the poles. I break the pole into its two pieces and lay them side by side. I will reel the line up good and tight, then wrap a tie around the top of the two pieces securing them together. Then I take another tie and do the lower half of the two pieces. With the line reeled tight and the ties holding the two pieces together, I know I won't have a tangled up mess when it's time to go fishing again. That means I'm on the lake quicker and catching fish quicker ... and the cost is minimal!

*Dennis Temby*
*Midland, TX*

# Improve a New Spinning Reel's Drag

When you buy a spinning reel with a front drag, super tune the drag washers and the spool. First, remove the retainer from the spool and lay out the washers on a clean cloth. The washers are usually made of composite, metal and Teflon. Check the inside surface of the spool where the last washer came from and the bottom of the drag adjustment nut. Use a craytex stick or small piece of fine sandpaper on a pencil to polish out the spool and drag nut. Using fine sandpaper or crocus cloth, sand the metal washers to a fine finish. Complete the job by polishing all metal surfaces with jeweler's rouge. Replace the washers, applying a light oil (slick 50 works great) to each washer. Your drag will operate much smoother and you will increase the range.

*William L. McCabe*
*Napa, CA*

# Customize Reel Handles

This tip is a simple, inexpensive way to customize your reel handles to give you a cushioned, non-slip grip without changing the originality of your reel. Go to the stationary department at your local variety store and pick up a packet of pencil jackets. They are used by students for their pens and pencils, and by artists and draftsmen. The hollow foam tubes come in an array of colors and cost no more than a dollar or two per pack of five. Slide the foam jacket over your reel handle and trim the excess. It's that easy! You now have a soft, comfortable reel handle that offers a non-slip grip in any weather condition. It's also great for arthritic fingers. This tip works best with older model Ambassadeur casting reels and mostly fly reels (non-paddle style grips).

*Jeff Fee*
*Lancaster, OH*

# Rod Saver

Kids love to fish. Trouble is, they have a hard time holding on to rods and reels, especially when casting or reeling in fish. Fortunately, you can make a handy "rod saver" from an inexpensive nylon dog leash. First, hook the loop end around the reel. Then slip the other end of the leash through the loop to tighten it. Finally, hook the clip onto the boat or other solid object, so if the rig slips out of his or her hands, you can easily retrieve it.

*Matthew Conway*
*Dracut, MA*

# Easy Rod Holder

To make a simple, inexpensive rod holder for wade fishing, just cut a pair of lengthwise slots, roughly 2 inches in length, in a short section of PVC pipe or similar plastic tubing. Next, simply slide it on your belt like you would a fillet knife sheath or similar holster-type item. This will allow you to use both hands to unhook fish, tie on lures, etc. without dropping your rod.

*Joe High*
*Afton, VA*

# Tighten Up Your Tennessee-Style Spinning Rod

Anyone who has ever fished a Tennessee-style spinning rod knows that the reel seat does and will come loose. One solution to this problem is to wrap the locking rings, reel seat and cork handle with electrical or Tommy tape. While this works well in solving the problem, it raises two other problems. The first, to remove the reel, for storage or travel, you must remove and replace a lot of tape. Second, by covering the cork handle with a waterproof material, you defeat the purpose of the cork, which is to absorb moisture and to keep your hands dry while fishing. My solution to this problem was to take 2-inch wide duct tape and wrap the section of the cork handle where the reel seat had compressed the cork. This allows the rings to be pressed on and taken off for storage or travel and leaves the cork handle exposed on each end of the compression rings. The duct tape, for whatever reason, doesn't allow the compression rings to clip or move like the cork does.

1. Remove reel from cork handle.
2. Start and end tape wrap where reel will sit on cork handle. This will make sure that the tape will not unwrap or leave the tape end to become sticky in the palm of your hand.
3. Wrap 2 layers of tape on handle and replace reel.

*Jim Whitenack*
*Muncie, IN*

# Back That Superline

When loading a reel with a superline, use a short length of light monofilament as backing. The inherent stretch in mono will help keep the superline tight on your spool, increasing casting distance and eliminating problems with the line burying itself into the spool.

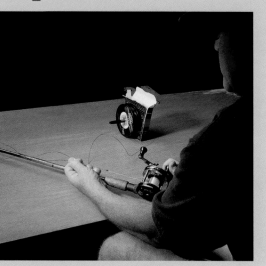

*Steve Pennaz*
*Executive Director, North American Fisherman*

# Slip-Bobbering is Effective

You don't have to live on Lake Mille Lacs in Minnesota to know that slip-bobbering is one of the most effective ways to fish walleyes on shallow rock reefs and in the weeds. Choosing the proper hook can substantially increase hooking ratios. A hook style that lends itself to a vertical hookset is critical.

When fishing floats for walleyes, a No. 10 wide-gap hook is ideal. The open sprout on these hooks offers the best possible bite on vertical hooksets. Wide-bend hooks enable the angler to select a smaller hook size than normal without sacrificing hooking or holding power.

Some anglers substitute a small leadhead jig for wide-bend hooks. The jig doubles as a hook and weight to keep the bait positioned at the desired depth. A crappie-sized ($1/32$- or $1/16$-ounce) jig tipped with a lively leech or minnow has accounted for many walleyes when fished in combination with a slip float.

The best jigs for float fishing have the hook eye positioned out of the top of the leadhead. A hook eye on the top keeps the bait resting in a natural, horizontal position.

## Follow This Tip

Have you ever been on the water, casting, only to watch your rod tip follow your lure into the lake? Next time you're on the water, make sure you have a butane lighter in your tackle box. When your tip top flies off, here's how to put it back on.

Line it up with the other guides (eyelets) and heat it up with the flame of the lighter. This will melt the glue around the tip top and should keep it in place until you can fix it more permanently. You'll be ready to start fishing again within 2 minutes.

*Terry Brodsky*
*Minnetonka, MN*

# Braided Lines Can Damage Tackle

I own a rod and reel repair shop and have noticed an increase in the number of reels spooled with braided line that have torn up pinion gears and stripped main drive gears. One Ambassadeur 5500C-3 even had the anti-reverse cog wheel broken loose from the shaft! When the reels came into my shop for repair, they all seemed to have the drags fully tightened down. When you set the hook on a fish, three things typically happen to take the force off the reel: The rod bends, the anti-reverse feature slips and the mono line stretches. When you use braided line, however, you transfer much of the force of the hookset directly to the reel's drive gear, anti-reverse mechanism and pinion gear. For that reason, I would suggest that NAFC members use a lighter rod when fishing braided line. Also, do not set the drag so tight—let it slip a little to relieve the pressure of the reel.

*Jim Stanford*
*Shreveport, LA*

# Rod Handle Repair

There's nothing like the feel of a fine rod handle made of Portuguese cork, but cork is not quite as durable as EVA foam. Often, chunks of cork get chipped away from the handle. Not to worry! To repair a cork rod handle, simply grind up the corks from bottles, etc. Mix the epoxy and fill in the holes. When the mixture has dried thoroughly, your rod handle will be as good as new.

*Steve VonBrandt*
*Wilmington, DE*

# Rod Protection

Protect your fishing rods when traveling by making homemade rod cases that are virtually indestructible. Visit your local home improvement or plumbing store and pick up some 3- or 4-inch diameter PVC pipe that is long enough to hold your longest 1 piece rod. You'll also need a matching cap and top, along with PVC cement. Glue the cap permanently with PVC cement and let it dry according to the instructions. Place your rods in the holder, secure the top with duct tape and you're ready to travel. After speaking with an airline baggage handler who has seen it all, including the best manufactured travel rod cases, PVC is the only rod holder material that he hasn't seen destroyed.

*Terry Brodsky*
*Minnetonka, MN*

# Taking Care of Tip-Ups

To prevent wooden tip-ups from freezing up, disassemble them and put 2 coats of urethane on the wood. When assembling, put small washers in between your crossbars before putting your screw bolts on. Never a freeze up and folds beautifully.

*Gerald Davis*
*Milanville, PA*

# Chapter Seven

## 7
# EVERYTHING FISHING

**S**ometimes it seems there's no end to the equipment you have to have, and the preparations you have to make, to go fishing. There's both good and bad in that, but one constant remains: Once you're on the water, you have to have a strategy to follow, and techniques and tactics to put into play, to catch fish. If you're fishing where the fish aren't, or using what they don't want to eat, well, you know what's going to happen. NAFC members know what they're doing out there on the water; here's their advice for better fishing, more often.

# Odor Removal

After cleaning fish, wash your hands with shaving cream to remove the odor.

*George Dougherty, Jr.*
*Belle Plaine, IA*

# Frugal Spooling

To save money and line when changing fishing line, take only half off the spool and use duct tape to secure what is left on the spool. You only throw away what was old and used.

*Keith Sadowski*
*Boynton Beach, FL*

# Successful Netting

Have you ever wanted to net a fighting fish but accidentally missed because the hooks from the lure got tangled up in the net because it was hanging so low? To solve this, take a woman's hair band or a small, thick rubber band and wrap it around the handle. Pull the net through so it is flat. When the fish is in the net, the weight of the fish causes the bag to pull free of the hair band and the net opens up with the fish at the bottom.

*Jethro Frydrychowski*
*Loudenville, OH*

# Net Woes

A problem I encountered when I first started fly fishing was with the landing net hanging in a "net down" position behind my back, in the traditional way most fly anglers carry it. I found it annoying how the net constantly banged against my back and behind as I walked. The net would also swing sideways, sometimes hanging up on the brush. To remedy the situation, I purchased a belt-type rod holder, which I put onto my wading belt behind me. The net handle goes into the tube and the net itself sticks upward in front of my vest. The result is that the net is out of the way, doesn't move around much, and keeps the net fabric against my back so it can't catch on the brush.

*Jay Jacobs*
*Baldwin, NY*

# Clean Hands and Kill Germs

Keep instant hand sanitizer in your glove box. This is something nice to have when you get your hands messy and smelly from fish when you are cleaning them. Alcohol kills germs and gets rid of the fish smell. Now you can enjoy the leftover potato chips on the car ride home without them tasting like fish!

*Scott Murphy*
*Lacey, WA*

# Filleting

Fillets cook faster and more thoroughly than do pan-dressed catfish, and most people find that they taste better as well. Granted, you will waste a small amount of meat, but the convenience is worth the cost.

Step 1: With the catfish lying on its side, make an angled cut from a point just behind the head down to a point just below the fish's midline. Cut down to the spine, but not through it. Next insert the knife's point into the initial incision and cut through the fish's side all the way to the anus. If you have not gutted the fish, be careful not to puncture the gut.

Step 2: Insert the knife into the initial incision with the blade's cutting edge pointed toward the tail. Hold the head and slice the fish all the way to the tail, taking a slab of meat from the fish's side. Keep the blade parallel with and against the spine. You will be cutting through the rib bones, so expect some resistance. When cleaning larger cats, an electric fillet knife makes the job a lot easier.

Step 3: Either clamp or hold the fillet's tail-end with the skinside down. Cut through the flesh down to the skin, but do not cut through the skin. Turn the knife toward the fillet's head-end and, with the blade angling slightly downward, separate the skin from the flesh by running the knife (using a cutting motion) between the two.

Step 4: Remove the rib bones and the row of smaller bones that are set at a right angle to the ribs by slicing through the fillet around the rib cage. To reduce the fillet's fat (and contaminant) content, remove a thin strip of meat from the fillet's lower (belly) side. Remove any of the red lateral line tissue that you may find.

Step 5: Rinse the fillet under running water and toss it into a pan of ice water. Repeat the process in removing the fillet on the other side of the catfish.

## Super Scaling

This tip will help fellow members who scale their fish. I mostly use this on panfish. First you take your bluegill and place it tail first on the clip-type gutting board. Then you take a garden hose, put the nozzle on 'stream' and blow the scales off from the tail to the head. I have scaled 30 panfish in 5 to 10 minutes this way and did not get any scales on me.

*Paul Mulvin*
*Erie, PA*

## Fish Alert

How many times have you lost a fish, while dead bait fishing, because you couldn't tell if a fish took your bait or not? Here's a sure-fire way to know. Once your bait is on the bottom, place a small bobber on your line near the rod tip. When the bobber's gone you know a fish has visited.

*Dan Carlson*
*Two Harbors, MN*

## Skinning Cats

An avid catfish fisherman from Louisiana, my son has cleaned his share of cats. He taught me a way to skin them that is simple and easy. First, he cuts off all the fins, then beheads and guts the fish. After a thorough washing, he wraps them in freezer wrap and freezes them with their skins on. When it comes time to eat the fish, he simply places them in cool water just long enough for the skin to thaw, then he goes to work with his skinning tool or pliers. You'll be surprised how easily the skin peels with this method and you will never have freezer-burned fish.

*Lucy Baker*
*Star City, IN*

# Suspended Walleye: Follow That Food

It seems safe to say that food drives walleyes. Food in combination with structure and cover almost always spells walleyes. But, as Mike McClelland points out, "Walleyes don't have a chain hooking them to structure. Structure is good because baitfish and other food congregate around it, and the walleyes can operate as ambush predators. But they won't sit on a nice rock pile and starve to death."

When a substantial food source is located in open water, at least some walleyes will follow it. We were long ago introduced to the concept of suspended walleyes by pioneering fishermen on the Great Lakes and other expansive bodies of water.

McClelland has studied the subject of suspension and fished suspended walleyes throughout North America.

"What moves walleyes," he begins, "is a search for food. Any time you get a forage base that suspends—like gizzard shad, tullibees, whitefish, that kind of thing—a certain number of walleyes are going to suspend. In certain cases, like on the Western Basin of Lake Erie, a majority of the fishery is suspended.

"In a lot of cases," McClelland says, "you can find the suspended baitfish on your sonar unit, and the walleyes will be sitting under them, chowing down on the ones that die off or get slashed by other fish. That's why jigging spoons are so effective on these suspended fish; they are used to looking for that fluttering action falling down toward them. It's natural. Walleyes can get below these gizzard shad, like on Lake Erie, and it's like leaves falling constantly."

"Especially when you have other predator fish working the forage, like white bass," says McClelland. "They bust into the baitfish and stun a lot of them, and the walleyes can just pick off the dropping ones. Sure, they'll get right into the baitfish, too, but they don't always have to."

"Their lateral lines can pick up the struggle of a dying baitfish from a long way away," McClelland continues. "Then they just slide over and suck in an easy meal. That's why you can't always catch those walleyes on crankbaits, even when you're at the right depth. They're just not programmed to grab something moving by at 2 or 3 miles per hour. That's why guys get over them with jigging spoons and really hammer them."

"We've been watching this happen for 30 years," says McClelland. "Bob Propst grew up with it on McConaughy (a sprawling southwestern Nebraska lake). Propst was using downriggers, lead-core line and jigging spoons in 1955! He was staring at 40-foot water clarity in his lake with deep walleyes and suspended walleyes, and he had to come up with a way to catch them. Bob was using these new 'breakthrough' methods, including planer boards, more than 30 years ago."

"In some fisheries, including a lot of the Southern reservoirs," McClelland says, "most of your summer fishing will be for suspended walleyes. Sure, some fish will be on structure, but the suspended fish will always be there if you can find them. It's not hard; they show up easy on your locator. Then, just drop a jigging spoon down to them. Or, if you troll over them with downriggers, try slowing down and popping the downrigger release when you pass over the school. Sometimes, the action of your crankbait fluttering slowly upward or a spoon fluttering downward will trigger the fish into biting. But generally, they are in with such a bunch of food that they're not easy to catch. Feeding is so easy for them. They wouldn't be in the open water if the food wasn't there, so realize your lure is competing with a lot of other food for the fish's attention."

# Shallow Water Walleye

When the sun is high in the sky, many walleye fisherman move deeper. It is my experience, especially early in the year when the carp are spawning, that the walleyes can actually be found in very shallow water. The walleyes follow the carp to eat whatever the carp are kicking up.

*Matthew Gohman*
*Waconia, MN*

# Fishing Kids

Many of us have children or grandchildren that we enjoy taking fishing. Most children, in my experience, become bored and restless after a period of time of fishing. To take care of this change of focus for the child, and at the same time, continue to teach the child about the use of a rod and reel, always carry a spare rod and reel (closed face) along with a kite. I have enjoyed many hours of quality time with my own children by hooking a kit onto a swivel, using a $3^1/_2$-foot rod and a Zebco 202 reel to fly a kite when the fish aren't biting. My children had fun learning the value of setting the drag and good retrieve methods to bring in a falling kite, which is good practice for bringing in a fighting fish. Try it. Take a kid fishing today!

*Adell Underwood*
*Mt. Hope, WV*

# Fish Thawing

There is a correct way to thaw fish. A frozen fish should be thawed slowly. Either put it in the refrigerator for 24 hours before cooking or place it in cold water to thaw. If the fish is thawed too fast, the outside flesh may deteriorate while the inside is still frozen too hard to cook through.

*Jason Hilton*
*Telford, TN*

---

"I wish I had a 20-page thesis," says McClelland, "on the movements and habits of every major forage fish there is so I could better understand them. I'd like to know when they spawn, when they go to shallow water, when they suspend. That would eliminate even more of the guesswork."

"People are really starting to get on these suspended walleyes in places from the Minnesota side of Lake of the Woods to Lake Erie to down South," McClelland continues. "But they typically don't find them until midsummer, about July or August. We need to look at this thing a lot closer to see whether the suspended fisheries don't set up until midsummer or if they're there at other times and we're just missing them. We have a lot of work to do, but it will be interesting. I'm excited about the possibilities."

"You've got to realize that walleyes in different waters are different fish. They go where it's easiest to eat; that's all there is to it. And that's going to vary in different bodies of water. That's why there aren't any good rules about finding walleyes," says McClelland. "You find them where they are at the moment, and they go where they go to find food."

# Catching Bass

The following is my favorite tip for catching largemouth bass during the tough time of the year called "tourist season". I call it: Beating The Tourist Season and Catching Bass. When tourists flock to your favorite lake in June and July, and all of the homes on the shoreline seem to be inhabited by jet skis and water skiers, and the lake surface looks like a hurricane is in progress, and my favorite honey hole is awash with boaters—I still catch my share of traumatized largemouth and then some.

First of all, I find that this works best on natural lakes rather than reservoirs, mainly because I have not found a reservoir with very shallow shore lines and fixed positions docks. My main tactic is to get out of the bass boat and wade the shoreline. Although this tactic can work well from the boat if you can handle being in tight quarters. I find the areas of the lake that have a relatively high population of boat docks sticking out from the shoreline—like quills from the back of a porcupine—are best for catching large numbers of bass. These areas generally have non-floating docks all up and down the shoreline and most are supported upon horses made from either wood or metal. I search out the docks that are setting on wood horses. The reason for this is that they offer better cover for bass and they are generally in shallower water up to 6 feet deep. Sunny days are also a plus as they generally are more productive because the dock offers protection from the sun.

Wading is the way to go, so go get some good hip boots and a fly rod about 8 feet long. On the end of your level floating line, tie on an 8 pound leader about 4 feet long and use a #6 short shank bronze bait holder hook and no weight. Another rig that works is to tie 6 feet of floating fly line on the end of your spinning rod line then 4 feet of leader. The fly line works well as a bite indicator because the bass won't take much line at all. I prefer the fly rod because of its length. For bait there are several options, but the 3 that I find to be the best are: live night crawlers, Berkley Power Worm (plain or cut the flipper tail off and in a natural worm color) or Gen Larew salt craws. Find a public access point close to the docks you have chosen and wade in.

As you approach the first dock, stay as close to shore as possible and start flipping your bait to the lake side of the first dock horse, even if the water is only a foot deep. Some of the biggest bass I have caught came from this first horse. Strange as it may seem, the more commotion there is around your chosen docks, the better the fishing is. Don't let those people swimming off the end of the dock bother you, it seems that the bass have become acclimated to the commotion and you can get close enough to the horse that you will only have to use 10 feet or 12 feet of line to reach the outside of the horse. They also seem to sense that they are not in too much danger. Try and keep your presentation in the center of the shady area under the dock. Watch the line as the bass will often take your lure without much of a run because you have placed it right in their dining room. Catch and release the boats that are tied to the docks as well.

After fishing the first dock, move onto the second and third. If wading, find knee deep water then bend over and work your way under the dock. This saves time and a lot of wading back to the shore though most people will let you get out of the water and walk around their dock if you ask them if they are there.

I have caught as many as 22 bass in one 3 hour trip on a busy weekend in the middle of July. My mentors, David and Denny Peterson of Stow, New York, caught over 60 bass on a sunny Saturday in a 3 hour time span on Fourth of July weekend.

If you are fishing in a bass tournament you will have to be in a boat, and the only handicap here is the relative closeness of the docks. The lake that I worked this method on the best had lake lots only 90 feet wide and most docks had boats tied up on both sides and maneuvering area was tight.

Keeping a log for the first 2 years of using this method, I discovered that I was catching an average of 3 bass per hour of fishing time over the entire season through September.

The many bonuses to this technique include saving on boat fuel costs, less frustration with crowded conditions, making friends along much of the shore line, getting in more productive fishing hours than your friends who elect to fight the crowds and the waves on the water and at the launch ramps. Good fishing!

*Fred Carpenter*
*Tumbling Shoals, AR*

## Line Cutter

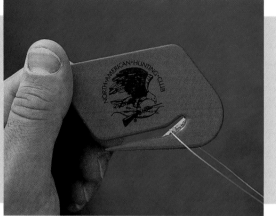

**I**f you want a small, inexpensive line cutter that will fit into your pocket, try a credit-card-size letter opener. They are sharp enough to cut a braided line.

*Steve VonBrandt*
*Wilmington, DE*

# Keys to Quickly Finding Fish

* Don't do a lot of fishing—unless maybe you troll while looking things over—until you see fish, or at least baitfish or other food sources. In deeper water, you'll have to rely on sonar; in shallower water, you can sometimes see fish, minnows being chased, freshwater, shrimp, frogs or other things.

* Don't spend a lot of time looking over, or fishing, a lot of the same type of territory. If you cast a lure around the rim of three lily-pad-filled bays and catch one small fish, don't go to a fourth lily-pad-filled bay. Look deeper, or in different kinds of weeds. Or in the open water of a deep basin. Systematically scope out different locations until you find a pattern.

* Even when you do find a successful pattern, don't assume it's the only one! Results of competitive bass and walleye tournaments have proven that a variety of fish-catching patterns can be "going" at once, on the same body of water.

* Until you locate fish and establish a pattern, fish quickly. In most cases, that means choosing a "horizontal" presentation that can be moved along: a live-bait rig or spinner behind a heavy bottom bouncer, a crankbait, or maybe casting a spinnerbait through high-percentage water.

* If you believe a slow presentation is the only way to tempt bites, don't spend all day trying it on the same spot. In that case, fish quickly by limiting the amount of time you spend at each stop.

* And now, the main rule of all: If things that should work don't, toss out all the rules and start looking where the fish shouldn't be, and start trying presentations they shouldn't be interested in. The open-minded approach has won a lot of money for tournament anglers, and it can save many a slow day for you.

# Early Ice

In general, wherever you find fish in late fall you find them at early ice. There is no mass movement, in other words, on the day ice forms. Pre-ice scouting in a boat is probably the most universally-missed opportunity in fishing. Many people in the "ice belt" store their boats for winter, taking care of that task before hunting season.

If you can hold off putting the boat away, spend a few hours on several lakes you want to ice-fish. Look for concentrations of fish on your sonar. Where, exactly, you look will vary slightly with different species, but typical late fall (first ice) locations are:

* Shallow flats that hold baitfish and insects. They should be near deep water. Many have weeds on them in summer. Many have flooded timber and brush, or other cover. In general, the bigger and more complex (having different depth levels, "stair-step ledges," and a variety of cover) the better.

Key winter fish-holding locations on larger flats are depressions and are easy to find with a depthfinder (many show on lake maps). If weeds on the flat get matted down, fish use water depth as cover.

* Steep drop-offs, that lead from these shallow flats into the deeper water. Some fish, but not all, will hold along the drop-off itself.

* The base of steep drop-offs, and the deep "basin water" leading off of them. Often, fish will spend time sitting in the deep water, moving up onto the shallow flat to feed. Or, they may suspend in the basin area. When fish are "resting," they are not looking for a meal, but can often be coaxed with a precise presentation.

You'll see fish on your depthfinder in the deep water and along the drop-off. But don't expect to see many in shallow water; your "cone angle" is so narrow in water of 10 feet and less that not many big fish stick around to be detected in it.

(Of course, not all bodies of water have structure like these. In waters with little structure, look for points and humps, even if they don't rise significantly. Anything that roaming fish have to "go around" will concentrate some, giving you better odds of putting a lure in front of a few.)

* For some fish, especially panfish, relatively deep (say, 30-40 feet) bays or basins with soft bottoms are the place to begin your search. Roam the basin with your sonar on, looking for groups of fish. Dave Genz of Minneapolis, Minnesota, who is fast becoming a legend in ice-fishing circles for his innovative methods and products, found a deep depression in a river backwater in the middle of summer, and

thought it looked like a winter panfish spot. Using county road maps, he found a way to drive through the woods right to the bank. The first time he tried the spot after freeze-up it was suspicion confirmed: sunfish and crappies for supper!

At the very least, identify high-percentage structure to return to. Get shore markings so you can find them easily after the ice forms.

The first-ice bite, as many already know, can be very good on these shallow flats. But the fish are extremely spooky (normally, there's no snow to mask your movements). If you're after bigger fish like pike, bass and walleyes, tip-ups—because you can back away and watch them—are often a better bet than jigging over the top of fish.

## Being Careful with Catfish

I go catfishing a lot and I hate to get stung by catfish fins, so when I catch them I place a large rubber band over their fins so I don't get stung. This often excites the fish and I make sure they aren't harmed by using Sure Life 'Please Release Me'.

*Steven Ondrejech*
*Altamonte Springs, FL*

## Ice House Heat

Here is a tip for making an ice shanty heater: Clean out a one-pound coffee can and place a roll of toilet paper inside the can. Fill the center section of the toilet paper with denatured alcohol. Let stand until alcohol absorbs, then light the top of the paper. This is very clean burning and has no fumes.

*Richard Johnson*
*Elida, OH*

***Editor's Note: Always practice safe measures when using fire.

## Holding Fish

When fly fishing on a stream, make sure that you fish all possible places where fish can hold. Many times trophy trout will lie in only inches of water. On several occasions, I have concentrated on fishing pools and riffles while wading through and supposedly, in the process, spooking at least 10 fish.

*Mitchell Masuda*
*Salinas, CA*

## Secure Sinkers

To prevent a split-shot sinker from sliding on the line, double wrap the line through the slot and around sinker. You don't need as much squeeze pressure to retain location on the line. This also prevents line damage, as some folks squeeze with pliers and weaken the line.

*Robert Kukuvka*
*Rockaway, NJ*

## Fish Handling

I use an old tube sock to handle my fish. It acts like a non-skid glove.

*Mark Nassis*
*Monroeville, PA*

## Cleaner Fish Cleaning

My tip would be to always wear disposable latex gloves when cleaning fish. The gloves come in a variety of sizes, so they can accommodate any hand size and they help you to hold onto the fish, which makes fish cleaning a breeze.

*Todd Fellman*
*Crystal, MN*

# Remove Those Scratches

Remove light scratches from your fish locater display face by rubbing it with a baking soda toothpaste.

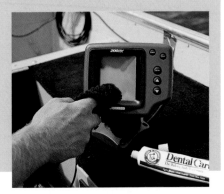

*Richard Johnson*
*Elida, OH*

# Warm Weather Fishing

Southern anglers, while being blessed with some of the finest fishing anywhere, are also cursed with scorching air and water temperatures in peak summer months. Fishing these high-temperature waters requires some extra steps to insure survival of your released tournament catches. I suggest carrying extra ice to cool live-well waters, proper aeration, prudent use of livewell chemicals and night fishing during the hottest months. Our club practices on further step: We assign members to take all fish out to deep, clean water for release. Do not release fish in canals with shallow, non-flowing water or near ramp areas that invariably have little or no oxygen content and tend to be fouled from excessive boat traffic. I hope this will help save some fish.

*Robert M. Rushing*
*St. Johns Bass Anglers*
*Jacksonville, FL*

# Look for Bass Under Algae

When a big amount of algae collects on the pond, usually at the beginning of spring and again in the fall, bass love to hide underneath the algae and hunt for food. The tip is to row your boat straight through the algae to clear a path. Then wait a few hours so the fish are no longer startled. When you return to the cleared area, cast your favorite lure down the path and retrieve it. Hold on tight!

*Martin Earhart*
*Charlotte, NC*

# Re-Spooling Strategies

If you fish a lot and find yourself re-spooling several times a year, I have found that it is best to start with the smaller pound test line early in the year and gradually increase your test as the year progresses. Being an avid walleye fisherman, I usually start with 6-pound test in the spring, when I am fishing smaller lures and making more finesse presentations, and end the open-water season with 10- to 12-pound test in the fall when I am fishing larger lures—match the hatch.

*Sean Gohman*
*Waconia, MN*

# Retrieving Lost Items

Drag the lake bottom with a stringer for retrieving lost items. If you lost something overboard, try grappling for it with a chain fish stringer. Tie the stringer to a stout cord, open the snaps and drag it back and forth over the bottom where the lost object disappeared.

*Jason Hilton*
*Telford, TN*

# Fishing from Shore

Not all fishing is done from a boat. In fact, it is my guess that people who fish from shore outnumber boat fisherman by at least two to one. Accordingly, this tip is designed to tell you how to catch fish while standing on *terra firma*, whether it be from a beach, the bank of a river, a bridge, pier, jetty, trestle, bulkhead or breakwater. The basics of fishing are the same no matter where you decide to try your luck. Use the same tackle used in boat fishing. Bait up in the same way, cast your hook into the water and land a fish. We advise you to arm yourself with spinning rods and reels. But there is one more item to arm yourself with: a cane pole.

To use a cane pole, rig it with a 10- to 20-pound test line and tie it off one quarter of the rod's length away from the tip. Wind the line in broad bands toward the tip and knot it securely at the very end. These broad windings act as do the guides on your spinning rod and distribute the pressure of a fighting fish across the weakest part of your pole. The length of your working line should not exceed the length of your pole; if it does you'll end up with more slack line than you can handle. Put a hook on the end and a pinch of shot or a bobber a few feet above it and you're ready for action. Bait up with a bread ball, worm, minnow or shiner. Drop the line into the water, take off your shoes, lean back in the shade of a tree, brace the pole between your toes, and live like Tom Sawyer and Huck Finn. When a fish nibbles on your line, just heave back, flip it up onto the bank and go back for more. Now that's shore fishing. Standing on a man-made structure is shore fishing too—and a grand way to shore fish.

*Leo Seffelaar*
*Broadview, Saskatchewan, Canada*

# Makeshift Trolling Motor

If you want to troll, but don't have a trolling motor, just tie a rope to the handle of a ten gallon bucket and then tie the rope to your boat. This way you should always be able to troll, even with powerful engines because the bucket will slow you down to a fish-catching speed.

*Justin Brinks*
*Wyoming, MI*

# Threading Line

With cold and stiff fingers, along with poor eyesight, I find it very difficult to thread braided line through the eye of a hook. So I use a needle threader and it does the job for me—it can be purchased at fabric or department stores.

*William Biacco*
*Oakdale, PA*

# Keep Fish Fresh Without Ice

I would like to pass on some helpful information to fellow members. The best way to keep fish fresh is to put them on ice, but I don't carry a cooler on my back while stream fishing. I use moss, green weeds or newspaper. These materials breathe, and if kept moist the evaporation will help keep the fish cool. You should also consider field dressing your fish as you catch them. Simply remove the internal organs and gills.

*Mark Breton*
*Anchorage, AK*

# Which Bite Day: or Night?

**M**any anglers argue over the ideal trolling motor; others disagree on the best times to structure troll. An effective presentation, trolling crankbaits over bottom structure has no limit during the day or after dark.

Most anglers would agree that walleyes bite better early and late in the day. However, these same fish are just as likely to bite during the middle of the day, if the environmental conditions are right.

Wind and wave action influence feeding times for walleyes more than the time of day. When the wind whips the surface into a chop, the chop reduces the amount of light that is penetrating the surface.

Low-light levels favor walleyes that see best in dim light, while baitfish that see best in bright conditions are at a disadvantage. Naturally, walleyes quickly take advantage of any opportunities when it comes to finding an easy meal.

Certain bodies of water offer either a better day or night bite. In general, fisheries featuring very clear waters often produce a dismal daylight bite. Fishing after dark is often the only way to effectively approach walleyes in clear water.

Bodies of water with significant boat traffic are also prime candidates for night-fishing. Ski boats, jet skis and other recreational crafts often churn up the waters of popular fishing lakes and rivers like a blender mixing daiquiris. On the most popular waters, only at night does the lake activity calm down enough to allow walleyes and other predatory fish to feed undisturbed.

Even fisheries providing dependable, daylight trolling bites often yield better fishing once the sun sets. Walleyes are opportunistic feeders. Under the cover of darkness, these predators go on the prowl. With their oversized eyes walleyes can see many species of baitfish that can't see them after dark.

This is why walleyes are normally more active early and late in the day. Low-light hunting conditions favor the walleye. Despite the fact that walleyes are less wary and easier to catch after dark, however, very few anglers fish the graveyard shifts.

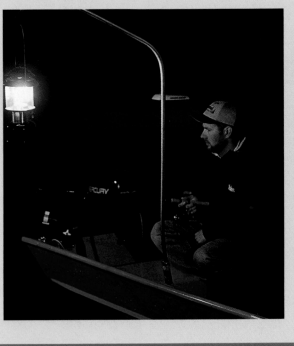

A lake, river or reservoir, familiar as your backyard, suddenly becomes an intimidating place after dark. Developing confidence in night-fishing takes some time. Like any activity, practice makes perfect. This is especially true when fishing in the dark. Even minor tasks become amazingly difficult.

Most dedicated night trollers outfit their boats with battery-operated lamps that provide enough light to accomplish basic tasks, such as tying on lures or sharpening hooks. Black lights illuminate the immediate work area; yet they aren't so bright that nearby fish are warned of approaching danger.

## Fish Keeper

I try to keep a gallon jug of frozen water handy in my boat cooler. I put fish on ice. The jug will stay frozen most of the day. Refreeze the jug overnight for the next day or keep extras for very hot weather. I have filleted fish right out of the water putting fillets on ice in a plastic bag. Keep in a separate container for disposal later on shore. When I get back to shore, the fish are perfect for the table or freezer and the work is all done!

*Stephen Turnis*
*Dubuque, IA*

## Fishing Log

Make a log of the fish you catch—what size they were, what lure you caught them on, where you caught them, water and air temperature, weather conditions and the water color. When you go out to that lake again, you will know what bait to use based on the conditions of where you are fishing.

*Sean Merritt*
*Sugar Land, TX*

# Importance of Record-Keeping

Catching bass is a rather simple proposition. Find the food and the best habitat option and you will most likely find fish. Execute the right presentation based on the details of the situation and the existing conditions, and you'll more than likely catch them.

By applying knowledge of the bass' seasonal behavior patterns to the available habitat and forage combinations, the task of narrowing the general location options becomes a fairly straight forward matter. Focusing on the existing conditions as they relate to the recent weather trends helps an angler choose appropriate presentations to the expected activity level of the fish in the positions judged to be worth investigating.

Haphazardly experimenting with a string of unrelated, narrowly applicable presentation/location possibilities is both time-consuming and frustrating. But conducting a logical sequence of experimental probes (casts/retrieves) can lead NAFC Members to the solutions.

By keeping track of the conditions, the steps taken in eliminating unproductive combinations of location, position and presentation, and the success or failure of those steps, anglers can build their own, personal knowledge base of bass behavior. It's that knowledge base that becomes the guide in expanding bassfishing horizons.

Recording all this is an important step in the "higher education" of bass fishermen. To gain maximum benefit, more than a common fishing log is needed. The approach and passage of weather systems should be recorded daily, as well as the less obvious changes in the aquatic world that stem from or relate to those changes in weather, lunar forces or anything else. The discipline of maintaining these records forces one to take note of the natural cycles and the weather. The eventual goal is to become so familiar with these factors that they are felt as they happen and there is an awareness of their impending arrival, as well as an awareness of the likely effect on the aquatic ecosystem without having to refer to the notes or log.

# Finding Dependable Night Bites

The nighttime walleye bite is a common phenomenon that anglers can tap into throughout the nation. Although walleyes can be caught after dark in almost any water, certain fisheries are better for night fishing than others.

"Strangely enough, lakes, rivers and reservoirs that provide dependable daylight bites aren't always the best night fishing waters," Tom Irwin says. "Typically, these fisheries contain huge numbers of baitfish, and walleyes have no problem finding enough to eat. Fishing after dark doesn't necessarily increase your odds of catching fish on this type of water."

Bodies of water that are subjected to many daytime recreational activities such as water-skiing or powerboating are excellent nighttime fishing prospects. During the summer months, the only time many of these waters are tranquil enough for walleyes to feed freely is after dark.

Natural lakes with lots of weed cover or sunken timber are also good prospects for night fishing. "The heavy cover provides baitfish with a maze of escape routes," says Irwin. "During daylight, walleyes instinctively know that they're no match for darting baitfish and young panfish. Once darkness arrives, the tide is turned and walleyes put their nocturnal hunting advantage into effect."

Fisheries that feature exceptionally clear waters are also good candidates for night fishing. "Super-clear water tends to make walleyes somewhat reluctant to feed actively during the day," explains Irwin. "The Sturgeon Bay area of Green Bay (on Lake Michigan) is a prime example of a clearwater nightfishery. The water in Sturgeon Bay is so clear it's tough to approach these fish during the day without spooking them. At night, this fishery absolutely explodes with angling opportunities."

Little Bay de Noc in Michigan's Upper Peninsula, Lake Erie's eastern basin, Lake Oahe in South Dakota and Lake McConoughy in Nebraska are just a few more examples of clearwater fisheries that support fantastic night fishing opportunities. No matter where you fish for walleyes, opportunities for nighttime walleyes exist.

# Lighted Fishing Net

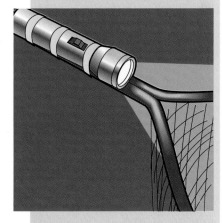

Duct tape a flashlight to the handle of your fishing net when night fishing for walleye, or any other fish for that matter. Not only will it help you land your fish, but you will always know where your flashlight is if you need to re-tie your rig.

*Matthew Radzialowski*
*Wixom, MI*

# Prevent Corrosion

Apply petroleum jelly (Vaseline) to threads on pork rind jars to prevent corrosion and to make removal easy.

*Robert Kukuvka*
*Rockaway, NJ*

## Ice Fishing Crappie Light

**S**ilicone a new car "bulb type" replacement headlight in a small glass jar. Attach the other end of a 6-foot cord to a small 12 volt battery. If the jar is too big, it will float. Use a rubber band to attach pencil sinkers to the jar to keep it down (if necessary). It's a great way to attract crappies to your hole while ice fishing.

*Matthew Radzialowski*
*Wixom, MI*

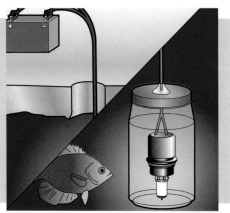

# Late Ice

**F**inally, the weather warms enough to start melting the snow and top layer of ice. (Ice also melts from the bottom up, especially in shallow bays.) The still-frozen lakes get sloppy, with standing water all over. When you drill holes to fish, water runs down the hole and into the lake. You're into the late ice period.

Soon, much of the standing water is gone. What happens is the ice breaks free from the bottom along shore and the whole ice pack, being lighter than water, "floats." You get open water, in fact, along dark-bottomed shoreline stretches.

You have to be careful and use common sense about your ice-fishing plans at this time of the year. The ice gets rotten looking, or "honeycombs" as they say. You can often punch through 8 or 10 inches of ice with a 2x4.

Good clothing is important for enjoying ice fishing all winter, but it can save your life at late-ice. This includes Mustang's anti-exposure coveralls. They are comfortable and warm, and an ideal cold weather, open-water fishing outfit. It doubles as your personal flotation device while boating.

As long as the ice stays safe, the fishing gets good again. The action of the ice pack being lifted by rising water levels uproots frozen-in vegetation and insects. This can happen in any depth that supports standing weeds through the winter. (Frozen-in weeds have been seen as deep as 12 feet.) That, warming water, and increasing oxygen levels attract fish to shallow water zones again.

Many fish are staging near spawning areas, and the fishing can be excellent, where seasons are kept open. Keep catch-and-release in mind.

## When to Use the Jerking Technique

"**I**t's kind of an ace-in-the-hole tactic that can help you out when nothing else is working." says Larry Williams, bass pro. "But it's most effective under a certain set of conditions."

"First, there needs to be a bright sun to warm the shallow water and bring up the bass. Next, you need some wind, because if the water is like glass, the bass will spook before you can get near them. Then all you need is a good, shallow flat and you're in business!"

Perhaps the real beauty of this technique is that it's well suited for that particular weather phenomenon notorious for sending anglers home with nothing more than a good excuse: the cold front. Warm air turns cold, water temperatures drop, the wind switches around to the north-northwest, and cloudy or hazy skies become bright blue.

"Many people think this drives the bass deep and turns them off," says this part-time pro angler from Lakeview, Ohio. "While that may be the case for some fish, others will be looking for relatively warm water. And they'll find it in certain areas of the lake where the shallows are sun-baked and maybe sheltered a little from the wind!"

## Money Saver

**S**ave money on fishing line. Don't fill the reel all the way up with new line. Fill it half way with old line, then tie on your new line. You will save 50 percent on new line.

*Bill Stalego*
*Newark, OH*

## Anise Attractor

**I** keep a small bottle of Anise oil in my tackle box. If you get gasoline or motor oil on your hands or equipment, just rub a few drops on your hands, lures, etc. Nothing repels fish faster than petroleum. I know some guys who use it as an attractor also.

*Kevin P. Studley*
*Port Richey, FL*

## Catch-and-Release

**I** do a lot of fishing in the surf and I release most of the fish I catch. I use freshwater hooks because occasionally I catch a fish that is hooked in such a way the hook cannot be removed without causing extensive damage to the fish. Therefore, I cut the line close to the hook and the freshwater hook will rust away in just a few days, whereas the stainless steel or other saltwater hooks will stay in the fish for an extended period of time. I have no proof but I believe a fish is more likely to recover with a freshwater hook embedded in it for a few days than a saltwater hook.

*William E. Pope*
*Alexander, AR*

## Garbage Bag Poncho

**T**his idea came to me when I wanted to go fishing in the rain when I had no raincoat. All you need is a garbage bag, pen, and pair of scissors or razor knife. First, lay garbage bag flat on a hard surface. Then draw a hole that you think will be big enough for your head and two for your arms. Cut the holes with the scissors and throw away the cut outs.

*Doug Wesserling*
*Dearborn Heights, MI*

## It's Not Too High To Fish

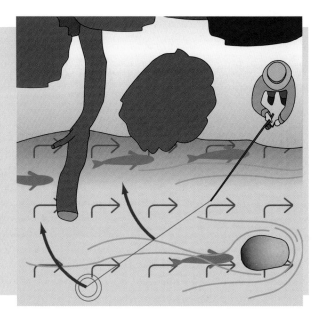

**W**ater ripping, discolored, too high to fish early in trout season? Take a #2 or #3 spinner ("french" blades are best) and fish tight to the bank. Take your time, cast quartering downstream a short distance and allow the spinner to sweep up against the bank below you. Your fishing about a 18-inch zone from the bank out. If the blade is turning, you are fishing. Allow it to hold in the zone for awhile, drop it back a bit, hold again. No strike? Reel in, move downstream a bit and try again. Take your time. Pay particular attention to pockets and slack water.

*Homer Lee*
*East Stroudsburg, PA*

## Baby Wipes Aren't Just for Babies Anymore...

**I** discovered a great way to clean your hands when fishing—use a baby wipe. In case you're not a new parent, they're available at discount stores and supermarkets everywhere. I buy the handy travel packs—they're cheap and easy to stash in my tackle box, and ready to clean my hands at a moment's notice.

*Jef Long*
*Derby, KS*

## Camo Net

**S**pray the handle and hoop of your landing net with flat-finish green and/or brown paint. This way the bright aluminum won't spook hooked fish at boatside.

*Robert Minch*
*Marion, IN*

## Bass Attractant

**T**o attract bass, take a piece of aluminum foil or tin foil and tie it so that it dangles over the side of the boat and hovers over the surface of the water. It will attract bass to that spot because bass are curious. You will have all the bass you want.

*Richard Johnson*
*Elida, OH*

# Finding Walleye in Rivers

Currents can flow in lakes when the wind kicks up. But currents are a fact of life around the clock for walleyes in rivers. Current, in fact, dictates much of what river walleyes do and where they go. To generalize, they try to hold just out of heavy current and feed on things that wash down to them, like trout or smallmouth bass do in the same environment. Many rivers also have backwater and slack water areas with minimal flow.

Throughout North America there are countless rivers, great and small, that hold walleyes. Many have dams on them, but because they are otherwise closed systems (without numerous smaller rivers or tributary streams flowing in), they are not considered reservoirs. We can also probably generalize that a river has a stronger current than a reservoir—although there are lazy rivers and portions of reservoirs with occasionally heavy current. Speed of current and maximum depth vary considerably (think of the Mississippi as opposed to a small backcountry river), but walleye movements are similar in most rivers.

As spawning time approaches, river walleyes do the same thing they do in reservoirs: move generally upstream toward suitable spawning habitat.

While many fishermen concentrate their efforts right below a dam (where legal), good fishing can also be found farther downstream. Numbers of walleyes do not spawn in the tailwaters, choosing rather to deposit their eggs in shallow areas that could be several miles downriver.

Gravel bars, rocky shorelines, and riprap dam facings are prime spawning grounds, but walleyes have been known to lay their eggs on flooded vegetation if nothing else is available.

As it is in lakes and reservoirs, female walleyes tend to leave the spawning area earlier than do the males, which can remain for up to two weeks. But, in general many post-spawn walleyes settle into nearby shallow water to rest, if you believe conventional wisdom, and feed. During late spring, the shallows are where warming temperatures and food are found. Some walleyes will be found in deeper holes downstream from spawning areas, but today's pro fisherman seeks out shallow, feeding fish.

Look in back bays, flooded trees or brush, or any shallow foodshelf out of the main current. Crowds of boats will always be around the dam, and so will a certain number of walleyes; don't be afraid to strike off a mile or two downriver looking for potential spots. Away from crowds you'll find just as many fish, and they'll be less pressured. (But shallow walleyes are easily spooked; approach them from deep water and make long casts.)

After the immediate post-spawn period, river walleyes settle into "key fish-holding territories," says Daryl Christensen who made his mark as a river guide and continues to do well whenever tournaments are held on rivers.

Christensen classifies two groups of key spots:

* Backwater areas-edges of, and right in, shallow-water sloughs, where walleyes can run in, feed and run back out to the main river. Also, any flooded willows, brush or other cover. Walleyes that feed in these areas can often be caught in the slightly deeper areas adjacent to them.

* Traditional summer locations-anywhere current is slowed for any reason. Bends in the river, sandbars, points, fallen trees, undercut bands, bridge pilings, wing dams, piers. Walleyes will hold on the slack side of the current break and dart out to grab food washing by. These

areas will remain good spots throughout the summer.

A special note: Don't just fish the downstream side of current breaks. Especially on wing dams, work the front face with a heavy jig. Depending on depth and current flow, it often takes ½ ounce or more to sink through the heavy current and into the slack water along the bottom at the front facing. Once the jig settles to the bottom, slowly work it parallel to the structure, back to the boat. Active walleyes often hold there, first in line to catch food coming by.

Also, there are often more potential spots than walleyes. Look closely for the presence of baitfish on sonar, or for those breaking the surface. They can be the clue as to which areas walleyes are using.

Fluctuating currents can dictate walleye location during summer. "Increased or decreased flow makes these fish move all the time," Christensen says. "When the water starts to drop, they move down current looking for holes to hide in. Begin fishing the upper end of these pools because many times walleyes will be there waiting for food to wash over the lip."

"If you get a lot of rain and the river rises, you can get an upstream migration of fish toward the dam," Christensen continues. "Any increase in current can stimulate walleyes to move upstream into the flow."

"That can make the dam a great summer spot, because it's a dead-end area that collects fish," he says. "They mill around, find plenty to eat and can provide super fishing for weeks."

As summer wears on and the dog days bring long spells of hot weather, walleyes use deep holes more. Shallow-water spots remain good, but vertically fishing jigs or live-bait rigs in deeper water (which could be 10 feet or 40, depending on the river) can pay off.

River fish, perhaps more than lake fish, pounce on just about any type of bait or lure, especially when they are holding on current breaks.

"A river fish is a more aggressive fish," says Gary Roach. "They can be a lot easier to catch than lake fish because of the current. If food goes by them, they have to grab it quickly or lose out."

As fall comes, walleyes again begin making that time-honored movement upstream toward spawning areas.

"We find in the fall that a lot of times walleyes make what we call a mock spawning run," says Christensen. "Especially if the water levels are not too low, you'll see fish staging in the pre-spawn staging areas, like they are about to go ahead and spawn. It doesn't always happen, but most of the time it does."

Many walleyes will winter in deep holes, especially on smaller rivers. Lots of walleyes will be around the dam, if there is one. But again, if you venture away from the crowds, you'll still find walleyes in a lot of the same places they were all summer. The keys are food and slacker water. River walleyes have to eat, and they don't want to fight the teeth of the current.

Finally, don't forget about the sauger when fishing gets tough. There are times when sauger can save the day if walleyes aren't active. The same techniques that work on walleyes will also take sauger; the difference is the latter are often found deeper than walleyes.

NAFC Charter Member, MWC tournament angler and river rat Gary Kiedrowski regularly fishes the Mississippi, and does extremely well on both walleye and sauger. When after sauger, he'll concentrate his efforts in waters 20 to 30 feet deep. But has caught fish as deep as 70.

"Saugers don't turn me on as much as walleye," says Kiedrowski, "but they are fun to catch when nothing else will hit. They can be aggressive little buggers, too!"

# Emergency Fire Starting

**C**arry a Ziplock baggy containing matches and strips of birch bark for emergency firestarting in wet conditions.

*Todd Fellman*
*Crystal, MN*

# Fish Beneath the Boat

**W**hen fishing for bluegills or crappie during summer, I move around quite a bit in search of the biggest fish. But when dusk finally settles, I stop moving and anchor. I take great care to remain quiet. The boat now resembles a piece of structure and roaming panfish begin to congregate right below. I find some of my best catches come from right beneath the boat. This works especially well during a full moon. Where legal, drop a waterproof fishing light into the water for even better results.

*Jonathan Storm*
*Senior Editor, North American Fisherman*

# Velcro Hook Cover

**P**revent hooks from getting snagged in your clothing—or worse—when carrying your rigged fishing rods in the car or boat. Purchase a ³/₄-inch wide strip of Velcro at your local sewing center and cut it into short sections. Wrap one of these strips around a hook or jig and you've got an instant hook holder.

*Fred Altrieth*
*Rochester, NY*

# Rain Protection

**A**lways carry a couple of heavy duty garbage bags in your tackle box for dry storage if it rains and/or for an emergency rain poncho.

*Todd Fellman*
*Crystal, MN*

# Catching Sunfish in Ponds

**P**onds offer excellent fishing for a variety of sunfish. Bluegills, redears and green sunfish adapt especially well to the small pond ecosystem, and in some areas, ponds may also have pumpkinseeds, redbreast sunfish, longears or other sunnies.

Many sunfish anglers shy away from ponds because they believe these diminutive waters aren't big enough to support good numbers of good-sized fish. But if you examine state-record bluegills listed, 23 (49 percent) were caught in ponds, including seven over 3 pounds and 12 between 2 and 3 pounds. Thirteen (52 percent) of the 25 state-record redear sunfish listed came from ponds, including three over 4 pounds, six between 3 and 4 pounds, and two between 2 and 3 pounds. Ponds also accounted for 50 percent of the state-record green sunfish, 50 percent of the state-record longears, and 29 percent of the state-record pumpkinseeds. Some poorly managed ponds are inhabited by tiny, stunted sunfish, but those with balanced populations of predator and prey fish can provide fast-paced fishing for heavyweight sunfish.

Though pond fishing exemplifies sunfish angling at its simplest and best, there's more to catching pond fish than just wetting a hook. Identifying the correct techniques, presentation, baits and locational factors is important even on these small waters.

Simply put, a pond is smaller than a lake, ranging from ½ acre to perhaps 25 acres in size. Ponds which can be man-made usually have such things as structure, vegetation and water clarity that can provide keys to catching fish. Pondwater may come from runoff, and underground springs or a feeder creek whose channel may be covered by the pond. Some are clear, others are muddy. Most ponds are also shallow so you can probe virtually every level.

Spawning season action starts sooner, because the shallow pond water warms more quickly than in large lakes. During this period, one simple method of fishing is to rig up a pole with a small, long-shanked hook, light line, a split shot or two, and a fixed bobber set at a shallow depth. Use worms or crickets for bait, and, walking the banks, look for fish congregated on their beds in shallow, sheltered water. Polarized sunglasses are a big help here, enabling you to better spot the dish-shaped nests and also helping you detect various forms of cover or changes in bottom makeup (rocks, gravel, weeds, logs, obstructions) that cause fish to congregate in those spots.

## Panfish Hook Remover

**T**ake a 6-inch piece of rib from an old umbrella and cut ½-inch slot in one end. Put slot over hook holding line taut. Then flip fish over and hook will turn out and fish will fall off hook. Works even with deeply hooked fish. Check for badly injured fish before releasing them as this method sometimes causes gills to be injured.

*Stephen Turnis*
*Dubuque, IA*

## Hat Saver

**T**hread one end of a 6-inch piece of small nylon twine or small wire through the pre-drilled hole in a medium-sized alligator clip, which can be bought at electronics supply stores very cheaply. Attach another clip to the other end of the twine. Simply attach one end of the back of the hat and the other end to your shirt collar. This has saved me many trips (and dollars) to the "hat store" and a blistered forehead.

*Martin McKee*
*Henryetta, OK*

# Locating Crappies at Night

Crappies might be located at night near their daytime haunts, but they're often a bit shallower. In spring, when crappies are shallowest, night fishing is least popular because the fish can be easy pickings in daytime. In summer on many lakes, though, night fishing becomes more popular and is an excellent way to beat the heat. Clear water crappies, especially, may be difficult to catch on a summer day, but they're more accessible to anglers at night. In summer, it pays to keep in mind the thermocline level. If it's 25 feet, they may be near this level. But, some fish are still bound to be shallower, especially at night. Fall and winter (including ice-covered lakes) can be great times to night fish with minnows or jigs. Think shallower in fall and deeper in late fall and winter.

To locate fish, look for fishermen, or search around woody cover, docks or bridges. You can call in crappies with lights, but it's best to check out an area first with sonar. Others set out brush piles at good nighttime spots and head straight for them. Some hang a sack of chum (where legal) such as bread to attract extra minnows around the sunken timber or concrete bridge posts.

Minnows can be fished vertically at night. Some anglers prefer to use a bobber, but currents or waves often float the bobber away from the crappie-holding spots. Jigs can be cast into the dark and very slowly retrieved into the light. Some crappies may hit at the illuminated area's edges (especially if the light is bright), and others right below the lights. One level is usually better than others, but that depth can change during the night. Keeping the sonar unit on alerts you to a change quickly.

Fishing is usually tops on dark nights, but even then, the action isn't at a constant pace. You may sit there an hour or two and not get a hit. But then at 10 o'clock, one in the morning or who knows when, you might run into all the night-owl crappies you can handle.

# *Secure Line with a Uni-to-Uni Knot*

An angler need not spool up with costly fluorocarbon to enjoy its benefits. When fishing clear water, especially the Great Lakes, I often use traditional monofilament line, or superline, with a fluorocarbon leader. Cut about 24 inches of fluorocarbon from a leader pack, then use a uni-to-uni knot to secure the fluorocarbon to the end of your main line. Now you have a camouflaged presentation without sacrificing your primary choice of lines.

*Jonathan Storm*
*Senior Editor, North American Fisherman*

## Light for Night Fishing

Wear a headlamp handy for night fishing. It's very helpful for tying knots, releasing fish or digging through tackle boxes at night.

*Dan Kennedy*
*Richfield, MN*

## Quick and Easy Wader Repair

How many of you have ripped your waders on the way to the river or lake? I have—and believe me, nothing can ruin a day of wade fishing faster than cold water pouring into your boots. But I've got a quick fix: Carry a plastic worm and cigarette lighter to repair the hole. Just heat up the worm and dab it in the hole or small rip to quickly fix your waders.

*Michael Rennie*
*Ogden, UT*

## No More Hooked Hands

If you dislike getting a treble hook in your hand, or dropping swivel snaps when you tie them, then just take a clothespin and place it on the hook or swivel to avoid getting into a mess. This works great because you have the whole unit to grab onto! Good fishing.

*Daniel Craft*
*Augusta, KS*

## Downrigging Attractants

A "scent" trick we use is to bore a 1/4-inch hole into the back of our downrigger ball, about one inch deep. A 2- by 1-inch piece of common household sponge can then be saturated with a fish attractant scent and pushed into the hole with a screwdriver. Leave about an inch sticking out, both to dispense the scent, and to allow easy removal. No need to refresh the sponge with scent for a couple hours.

*Jim Paige*
*Montpelier, VT*

## Portable Fish Cleaning Table

An ironing board makes a great lightweight, portable fish cleaning table.

*Ken Slowinski*
*Iron River, WI*

# Finding Open-Water "Basin" Fish

**A**fter top anglers taught many fishermen to find and fish structural elements, fish and structure became glued together in their minds. Find structure and you'll find fish. Fish are always "relating" to structure in some way.

The reality anglers have come to learn, is that fish often hold on or near structure, assuming environmental conditions (water temperature, oxygen levels and light levels) are favorable and food is found on the structure. "But," says Mike McClelland, "a fish doesn't say to himself, 'Boy, look at that nice rock pile; I think I'll go over there for a while.' He doesn't sit on a nice rock pile and starve to death. He won't be there unless his food is there."

Anglers have come to learn that much fish food is found in the middle of nowhere at certain times of year. They've learned, through the efforts of tournament anglers like Keith Kavajecz and Gary Parson, that a lot of fish—and big ones, too—can be caught by plying the open basin waters, sometimes miles from any structure.

These fish are sometimes called "suspended," but they can be on or near bottom. And anglers now think of them as completely disassociated from structure, but some of them are "structure" fish that have slid off, horizontally, from structure—either after feeding, to chase moving baitfish, or as a reaction to fishing or boating pressure.

But how in the world do you efficiently search for open-water fish, especially in places like the Great Lakes?

Parsons and Kavajecz have a system. Here are the highlights which will make you a better basin troller:

* Rumors about certain general areas that kick out a lot of fish can get you started in the right direction.

* Always have your sonar unit running, and keep your boat speed at a level that allows a readable display, as you move from spot to spot. Be looking for fish and baitfish as you cross basins. (A large bay can be a basin.)

* If you see fish, set lines to troll. Crankbaits are a good choice. Don't even blink while you purchase a copy of Mike McClelland's book *Crankbaits* and one of his *Crankbait Trolling Depth Guides*. They are the only sources of their kind. They tell you how deep more than 200 lures run, on different line weights, and with differing lengths of line out. You can set lines to a variety of depths, after choosing from a variety of lures with differing actions and wobbles. You don't know, ahead of time, what action will trigger strikes.

One important note: Always set at least one line to run shallow, about 3 to 6 feet. Even if you don't see any shallow fish on the depthfinder, they can be there. It's a deadly sin to ignore this possibility!

Now make trolling passes, the scope of which are determined by the size of the area

## Tools and Accessories

When you clip the tiny bells onto the tip end of your fishing rod, often times it falls right off into the water due to accidents (ie. sea gulls, pigeons hitting fishing lines, knocking your poles over to the side, etc.). Now you can save those bells by using a small piece of fishing line. Tie one end of the line to one side of the bells, and the other end of the line onto a small snap. When it's finished, you can now clip the bells onto the tip of your fishing pole as usual, then slip the snap in between the main fishing line and your pole. The fishing bells are now nicely and safely attached to your pole to detect any bite.

*Eddie Ong*
*Daly City, CA*

## Anchoring with Attractants

Before anchoring your boat to still fish, apply a small bead of your favorite fish attractant to the anchor rope, a few feet from the bottom. Often, we tie a small piece of rag to the anchor rope, for this purpose. "Natural" scents, such as crawfish, nightcrawler and smelt work best!

*Jim Paige*
*Montepelier, VT*

## Locating Crappie

If you are looking for crappie, use a baitfish or spoon either under a bridge or near the rocks. If you are fishing near the rocks, use polarized glasses and if you can find any holes, dip your lure or bait down into it and bring the lure back up. Jigging, bumping and simply retrieving quickly will usually trigger strikes. The larger the spoon, the larger the crappie that strike.

*Tracy Benton*
*Boca Raton, FL*

to be covered. Parsons and Kavajecz normally track their passes on the plotter function of a Loran-C unit. Then, as they make each successive pass, it's easy to run a parallel path.

These pros don't cover the same area twice, until they contact fish. When they catch fish, they record the location as a waypoint in their loran. In this methodical manner, they can actually chart the size and location of an open-water school of fish, which can be huge! They can stay with schools as they move on successive days, by first returning to the fish's previous location, then branching out in each direction until contacting them again-always keeping track of boat movements on the loran.

* Even if you don't have a Loran-C unit, or fish in an area where loran reception isn't good, you can try to be precise. If the area isn't too big, take shore markings and compass headings as you make each trolling pass. It'll help you avoid covering the same area more than once. When you catch fish, take shore markings again and write them down for your future reference.

# No Tangles Tackle Box

To keep snells from tangling in your tackle box, take a piece of foam insulation and wrap it around $1/2$-inch water pipes. The foam is big enough in diameter so the snell won't curl, yet it's soft enough to stuff in the box.

*Kyle Young*
*Fridley, MN*

# Too Much Line, Too Many Tangles

Pay attention to the maximum line yardage printed on your spools. Too much line on your spool often leads to unwanted knots, tangles and down time, since the excess line comes off the spool too easily.

*Joe Johnson*
*Apple Valley, MN*

# Locating the Thermocline

Through the years, Chris Altman, a catfish authority, has learned several ways to pinpoint the thermocline's location. "The easiest and most convenient method is simply using your depthfinder," he says. "By cranking up the sensitivity on your liquid-crystal unit or paper graph, you can usually see thermocline on the screen. Most often, the sensitivity has to be increased to the halfway point or higher before the thermocline becomes visible. On a liquid-crystal unit, it appears as a horizontal line across the screen. On a paper graph, it appears as a gray, hazy, poorly defined band across the paper." What the sonar unit is picking up, says Altman, is a "mud" layer that forms in the thermocline, rather than the actual thermocline itself. This "mud" consists of dead algae and plankton that has sunk to a depth at which the material becomes neutrally buoyant and then suspends. Most often, this occurs within the thermocline.

Another means of locating the 'cline is by using a portable temperature probe or one of the combination (temperature/color/pH) units now marketed. "These units usually have a probe suspended on a coaxial cable which is marked in 1-foot increments. By lowering the probe 9 feet at a time, you can actually map the thermocline by simply watching the temperature change on the unit's meter. When the probe reaches the thermocline, the temperature drops rapidly, about half a degree per foot of depth," Altman explains. "When the probe exits the bottom of the thermocline the temperature continues to fall, but at a much slower rate."

"Some successful anglers have learned to simply suspend their baits at about the lake's mid-depth point during the later-summer months. If they fail to get a bite at that depth, they'll begin raising their bait about 1 or 2 feet at a time until they find the cats," Altman says.

# Signal Light

A simple, low-cost way to convert your flashlight into a red, green or fluorescent signal light for boating and roadside emergencies is by using the cap from a spray paint container. The cans come in various sizes, so you should be able to find caps for almost any light. Keep them in your boat and tow vehicle.

*John Verichio, Jr.*
*Cape Coral, FL*

## Protecting Metal Files

**R**usty old metal files don't sharpen hooks well. One way of protecting a new file from getting badly corroded is simply using a leather knife sheath sprayed with a penetrating oil such as WD-40 or Corrosion Block to store your file in. Keeping your metal file protected in an oil soaked leather sheath will help keep it from rusting. Occasionally cleaning the file grooves with a wire brush, along with re-oiling the leather sheath season to season, will keep your file sharp and ready for use.

*Captain Del Dykes*
*Kailua-Kona, HI*

## Tracking Schooling Fish

**T**o follow active schooling fish, blow a balloon up and tie it off. Then tie a length of mono to the knot of the balloon. To the opposite end of the mono, tie a snap. When a schooling fish is caught, attach a clip to it and release. Then follow the balloon to the fish.

*Robert Owens*
*Baltimore, MD*

\*\*\*Editor's Note: This practice is illegal in some states. Check with your state's regulations.

## Still-Water Rigs

**T**o fish water having little or no real current, you must understand the theory of the "sphere of discovery." This is the distance at which the fish first can see, sense or taste your bait. Think of your bait as a peach pit and the sphere of discovery as the peach skin. Slice the peach in half and the resulting half is "hemisphere of discovery" for baits fished on the surface or bottom. If you cut most of the fruit away and jam the pit into a rocky-bottom crack. The sphere almost vanishes. If you float the pit a foot or so off the bottom, the area of water from which fish can be attracted to your bait radically increases. This is the reason air-injected worms or marshmallows work so well; they're a leader-length off bottom with a bigger discovery area.

Of course, if your bait's sphere of discovery sits in water that's too hot, too cold or, in the case of fish that stay put and ambush bait, too far from the right structure, you probably won't catch anything. There will be a difference in methods and movement around and on your favorite fishing water between species that cruise, like trout or salmon, and the more "stay at home" types, like muskies or bass, that ambush their prey.

In the first case, you can wait for the cruisers. Otherwise, try a few techniques or baits, then move to a new location if there isn't any action.

# Wing-Dam Tactics

**M**any large river systems, such as the Mississippi and Missouri Rivers, are lined with wing dams. Built by the U.S. Army Corps of Engineers, these finger-like appendages are actually linear rock piles that stretch from the shore out into the main current. Strategically placed, wing dams are designed to increase current speed through the main shipping channel.

Water striking these dams is deflected toward the middle of the river, increasing current speed and, in turn, forcing the river to carry its heavy load of sediment downstream. Wing dams help reduce or eliminate expensive dredging operations and keep shipping traffic moving smoothly.

Locating wing dams is easy. Many river maps clearly mark the location of productive fishing dams. Also, water rushing over the top of these linear rock piles causes an easily noticed boil on the surface. Any good fishing graph will also mark these structures as the boat passes over them. Anglers should be careful when navigating over the top of these dams. Some are covered by enough water to allow fishing boat traffic to move freely over them while others are prop-busting demons. It's safer to avoid running your boat directly over the top of wing dams.

Although wing dams weren't built with anglers in mind, they do provide a unique mini-habitat for many species of fish, including walleyes, sauger, smallmouth bass, white bass and catfish. Most fish found around a wing dam will be along the dam's front face near where the rocks forming the dam meet the river bottom. Known as the apex, this small slack-water area is formed when the river current collides with the dam face and is then diverted over and along the side.

Directly downstream from the dams, rolling, turbulent waters create a deep hole referred to as the "scour hole." Walleyes and other fish sometimes can be found in the scour hole, but these fish often are inactive and difficult to tempt into biting. The more active fish will usually be near the apex, or scattered along the front face and top of the wing dam.

Water levels and current speed dictate the walleyes' exact location. In high or swift water, the fish usually tuck in close to the bank where the current is a little slower. Small back eddies usually form tight along shore, providing ideal ambush locations for walleyes.

When the water level is normal, the fish spread out along the front face of the dam. Breaks in the dam or debris lodged against the rocks often concentrate these fish.

During extremely low-water periods, walleyes and sauger move toward the tip of the wing dam where the river is swifter and slightly deeper. Extremely active fish can also be found on top of the dam during normal and low-water periods. Casting a diving-style crankbait and retrieving the lure over the top or along the face of a wing dam is often an exciting and productive way to tempt active biters.

It's difficult to describe the perfect fish-holding wing dam. Most river experts agree that certain characteristics reveal whether a particular dam or series of dams will consistently hold fish. Wing dams located along outside river bends often attract excellent numbers of walleyes. This is because these bends naturally concentrate baitfish. If four or more dams are positioned along the bend, the action will be great. Several dams in close proximity deflect and reduce the current more than a single dam, creating an even better environment for baitfish and gamefish alike. The best wing dams in the series are usually those that are situated in the middle.

New dams that aren't laden with silt offer more cover for baitfish and, in turn, attract more walleyes. Also, long wing dams and dams that feature elbow-like bends can be top producers. Bends, breaks or other physical features along the wing dam concentrate fish.

Understandably, anglers who ferret out the best producing dams often are reluctant to share their findings with others. Still, certain dams become popular "community" fishing sites. Unfortunately, these popular dams are often poor producers because of the greater fishing pressure.

Successfully fishing wing dams is a challenging and sometimes difficult walleye-angling technique. Positioning a fishing lure along the front face of a wing dam requires extreme boat control. The angler who snoozes for even a moment loses. A steady flowing current can quickly sweep a boat downstream from the dam without the angler even knowing it!

Current near a wing dam is faster and acts like a powerful vacuum, sucking the boat over the dam and out of the fishing zone. Though there are several ways of fishing wing dams, most successful anglers position their boats upstream of the dam. Using a powerful electric motor or small gasoline outboard "kicker" to hold the boat in the current, they slowly slip back and forth along the face of the wing dam.

Keeping the boat's bow pointed into the current when backtrolling along the face of a wing dam is a lesson in futility. Strong currents colliding with the transom make boat control difficult.

A heavy leadhead jig or a Wolf River (three-way swivel) rig are the standard terminal setups for this type of fishing. Jigs are normally used in low to normal current, but a heavy, pencil-style sinker on a three-way rig works well in stronger current. A 24- to 60-inch snell with a single hook, spinner, floating jig head or shallow diving crankbait is normally attached to the three-way rig.

In some states, where it's legal to fish two hooks on one line, the Dubuque rig, a modified version of the Wolf River rig, is a popular river-fishing system. A large leadhead jig is substituted for the bell sinker or pencil weight on a Wolf River rig, allowing the angler a little fish-hooking advantage. Dubuque rigs are not legal in all states so consult local fishing regulations before using them.

Both jigging and rigging systems are baited with minnows, nightcrawlers or leeches, depending upon the availability of bait and the fish's interest. Minnows normally work best early and late in the year while 'crawlers and leeches are preferred for warmer weather.

"I feel strongly about bulking up my presentation with various plastic grub or action tail bodies," says Stan Berry. Berry and his partner Harry Stiles, teamed up to win the Masters Walleye Circuit World Walleye Championships.

"Bulking up a jig or single hook with plastic grub tails makes the overall lure larger and easier for walleyes to spot," explains Berry. "Plastic bodies also come in a rainbow of colors that help walleyes isolate bait in stained, dirty or off-color waters."

When fishing wing dams, the bait, grub body or terminal rig is usually less important than the accuracy of the lure presentation. Positioning a boat in front of a wing dam and dropping back downstream until a jig or three-way rig contacts the wing dam's apex is no easy task.

Unless the angler pays close attention to his boat-control chores, the lures will be washed up into the broken rock along the face of the dam where they are sure to snag. Lures positioned too far in front of the apex will be out of the primary strike zone, producing very few fish.

Successful anglers cautiously drop their lures back until they can feel the sinkers hitting the rocks at the face of the wing dam. Once the baits are in position at the apex, the boat is moved perpendicular to the current, and the lures are dragged along the face of the dam.

The technique sounds easy, but in reality it requires practice and patience to master. Expect to snag and lose a lot of tackle. Even a skilled wing-dam fisherman snags up frequently. If you don't snag up once in a while, your lures probably aren't close enough to the apex to tempt waiting walleyes.

Most anglers use an abrasion-resistant, 8- to 12-pound-test monofilament to keep the number of break-offs minimal. Both spinning and baitcasting tackle work for fishing wing dams.

Using a stiff action rod makes it easier to detect light strikes, because heavy weights are often used to keep the bait on the bottom. For thousands of anglers, finding and catching walleyes in rivers is the name of the game. Flowing water has much to offer the walleye angler.

# Anywhere, Anytime Matches

I think other anglers will find this tip useful. I like to keep matches in my tackle box (the strike anywhere type), and to make them waterproof I dip the heads of the matches in melted candle wax. This light coating proves to be beneficial for both fishing and camping and by using the strike anywhere type rather than the strike on box type, you don't have the problem of the wax building up on the box where you strike the matches.

*Gordon MacDougall*
*Ludington, MI*

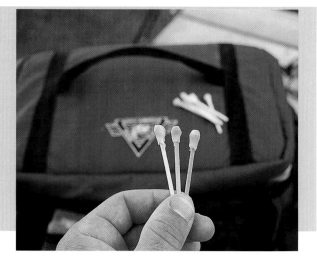

# Miniature Chum Pots

Chum pots are great. This is a small pot for still-fishing piers, bridges and fishing from small boats in bays. For many years I have used the following: a small can of the cheapest sardines in oil. Some fishermen have tried canned cat food, but I believe it is not oily enough. Solder a small ring on one end of the can, to fasten it to your fishing line, and shake the can vigorously before attaching to line to break up the sardines. If there is no current, use it in place of the sinker. Just before you drop it over into the water, punch holes in one side—four or five will do. If you punch holes in both sides you will have an oily mess on you, your gear and anywhere the sardine oil drips. This oil and bits of sardines will form a slick away from your bait for three to four hours. Remember to get the cheapest sardines in oil.

*Ronald Inch*
*Etobicoke, Ontario, Canada*

***Editor's Note: Chumming is illegal in some states. Check with your state's regulations.

# Drainage Pipe Fishing

For fishing trout along road sides, look for underground drainage pipes. Move slowly toward them then dip the bait in front of it. If a fish doesn't take it, there is no fish there. Then cast the bait into the pipe.

*Jeff Swarthout*
*Barryton, MI*

# Disable Disabilities

I am a serious angler who was able to fish wherever I wanted. Now I am paralyzed from the waist down and have discovered that it is difficult, even impossible, to enjoy much of the fishing that is available. Owning my own boat helps, but I really miss fishing local streams as I can't get near the water. Disabled anglers are people just like you and me and many would like to fish more often. I have recently found that many states and provinces across North America are working hard to increase opportunities for disabled anglers. If you are disabled, contact your local organizations to find out where accesses for disabled anglers are. Don't let any disabilities stop you from enjoying angling in the great outdoors!

*Trevor Jablonski*
*Kendall Park, NJ*

# Walleyes in the Weeds

**N**ot all walleye waters have weeds, especially reservoirs, where fluctuating water levels make it tough for them to take root. But where they are found, weeds—and weed edges—become a haven for walleyes.

Weeds offer walleyes food, comfort and security. There are plenty of hiding spots from which they can ambush baitfish, and the canopy provides shade, cutting light intensity and cooling the water.

But to a walleye, not all weeds are created equal. If given a choice they prefer the cover of broadleaf weeds, such as cabbage, over that of narrowleaf weeds, like coontail or milfoil.

Tournament veteran and long-time tackle promoter, Gary Roach, has fished more weedy lakes and has probably caught more weed walleyes than any man alive. He says that edges in the weeds come in various forms, from distinct outside and inside weedlines to pockets in dense growth.

"Anywhere you have weeds you have edges, and lots of 'em," Roach says. "I hate to harp on this subject all the time, but you need to learn to see weeds on a depthfinder, to find the weedlines. You'll find weed points, inside turns and patches where they grow thicker and thinner."

"Exploring the weedline is probably the best way there is to find your own spots away from the crowds," Roach says, "because these places never show up on a contour map. Don't be afraid to fish anything that looks good to you. Get a little adventurous and it'll pay off. Walleyes like to relate to those edges, and you'll catch a lot of them by carefully following them along."

Roach also points out a fact well known among tournament pros but often missed by weekend anglers. When most people think of the weedline, or weed edge, they think of the deep edge where the weeds stop growing before the bottom breaks off into deep water. But walleyes also hold on the inside weedline, the shallow-water area between shore and the first thick growth of fish-holding weeds.

"Many times," he says, "the inside weedline is as distinct as the deep weedline. Walleyes don't always hold there, but I make a point of checking it in the late evening, early morning and when the fish have been pressured by a lot of boats and fishermen."

The inside weedline is often visible, especially in clearer-water lakes. Shallow water holds lots of walleyes, and many big ones. But remember this credo of the pros: When fishing shallow, fish from a distance. Don't expect to motor up to an inside weedline and see fish swimming all over. Stay as far away as possible, making long casts with light baits.

The weedline is deeper in clear water, shallower in dirty water. That's because the sun can't penetrate the dirtier water as well, and the darkness chokes off growth beyond a certain point. The same thing happens in clear waters, but the weedline can be as deep as 25 feet in some cases. In dirty water, weedlines of six to eight feet are common.

So you're ready to attack the water and check out the weedline. One look down the shoreline tells you this could take years! It could, but Roach says there's no need for dragging it out.

"The thing I like to do," he says, "is get among the weeds and run pretty fast. I'm looking for little openings that indicate harder bottom (weeds grow well on organic bottoms and sparsely or not at all on sand or rock). I run in and out, shallower and deeper, with my depthfinder set so I'm just barely not getting a second echo when I'm over the softer bottom. Then, when I hit hard bottom, I instantly get a second echo and I can make a note of where I am."

"Just run down entire sections of weeds like this," Roach advises. "Sometimes I go fast with the electric motor, backtrolling with a jig or Roach Rig. I move down whole long sections of the weedlines, looking for points, inside turns, rock piles, just anything different from what's around it."

This isn't easy on a new lake, because there is a lot of ground to cover. And remember, weedlines aren't the only edges in town. In a lot of waters weeds may not even be present. Check out any kind of edge you find.

# Walleyes on the Edges

Food probably controls walleye location more than anything, except at spawning time. Consider for a moment the effect that edges have on the location of everything in nature, including walleyes.

Edges are everywhere, and their draw is almost magical.

The edge of a weed bed. The edge where soft bottom changes to harder bottom. The edge where a drop-off is most abrupt. The tip of a point. The edge of a timbered flat.

This is not to say that walleyes won't be found in the middle of a thick weedbed, because at times they will be. They will also be found in the middle of nowhere suspended near schools of baitfish or suspended away from structure, apparently resting.

But a lot of great walleye fishermen believe edges funnel and lead walleyes from place to place and collect them in prime feeding lies. So, finding edges can be the key to finding and catching fish.

Analyze the waters you fish. What sorts of edges are present? If they have very little classical structure such as rock piles, points and the like, there might be no edges except transition lines between bottom types. This is especially true of lakes with bowl-shaped basins, an environment where Gary Parsons, a member of Team Skeeter, shines.

"Even casual fishermen can learn to find these transition lines between soft and hard bottom," he says, "and they can be the key to locating walleyes a lot of days. Once you learn how to distinguish hard from soft bottom on a sonar unit, go out on any lake and find the depth of the transition line in one place."

"Now, the transition will usually be at that same depth all along the shoreline," Parsons continues. "Not always, but most of the time, you're going to have fingers coming out along the shoreline break, but a finger is nothing more than a pile of rocks or other harder bottom. I visualize mud or other soft, featureless bottom as being flat in most cases. The basin of the lake is normally pretty flat and uniform. I visualize structure, then, as anything coming up off that basin."

"So, all the way around that structure, if there is any, you have a fairly equal and uniform depth. It might vary a few feet, but if you find that transition line and it happens to be at 10 feet, or 25 feet, you can follow that depth contour and stay pretty close to the transition line."

Parsons knows that walleyes often sit right on that transition line. He and his partner Keith Kavajecz have made a science out of following it with their liquid crystal sonar, using the precision of the digital depth readouts to pinpoint the depth of walleye locations.

"The digital readouts are great; we love them," says Kavajecz. "Sure, they might not be as fast as the flashers, but they are easy to read and can really help you nail down depths. At the Otter Street MWC tournament one year, for example, we found that 9.6 feet was the right depth to troll. It wasn't 10 and it wasn't 11. Who knows, it could have been partly psychological, but it seemed to work. And it was easy to do with those big numbers to stare at."

# Chumming with Anchovies

**W**hen I use anchovies or sardines to catch stripers at Lake Mead in Nevada, I chum small pieces of anchovies in the water. One thing I like to do is use my oar as a cutting board and I can also use the oar to broadcast the cut pieces over a larger area in order to attract fish from farther away.

*Mike Carns*
*Henderson, NV*

***Editor's Note: This practice is illegal in some states. Check with your state's regulations.

# Pull the Plug on Fishing

**L**aziness breeds efficiency, so next time your fishing boat has a lot of water in the bottom, try pulling the boat plug after you're able to get up on a plane. Continue to watch the water drain, making sure you can see daylight between the plug hole and the water. Once the boat is drained, put the plug back in and start fishing. You might want to have your fishing partner pull the plug for you while you're safely driving the boat.

*Terry Brodsky*
*Minnetonka, MN*

# Beware of Tackle Thieves

**I** thought I'd pass on an experience that other members should be reminded of. I returned late one night from an all-day fishing trip to a local lake. Knowing I was going back the next day, I left my gear in the back seat of my locked car. The next morning, I awoke to find my car had been broken into and some of my gear was gone. The thieves had taken two of my fishing rods but luckily passed over my fly rod and tackle boxes. It seems they were only interested in stuff they could run with (the boxes weigh 23 pounds each). The lesson it taught me was to remove all gear from vehicles or boats when parked overnight. The few moments it takes to put your gear in a safe place may save you countless headaches. It pays to keep an eye on gear when shorefishing too. Don't wander too far from your tackle box for just one more cast—it may be gone when you get back.

*Gary McDougall*
*Penticton, British Columbia, Canada*

# Bail-Open Fishing

**W**hen live bait fishing from shore, I place a small rubber band around the rod handle just ahead of the spinning reel. Cast out, let the bait sink to the bottom, then slip a little line underneath the rubber band and leave the reel's bail open. When a fish strikes, the line releases. The rig even works well in windy weather, when other bail-open approaches invariably end in disaster.

*Chris Spencer*
*Schenectady, NY*

# Techniques for Shallow Smallies

Floating Rapalas and the Jitterbug are fishing guide Gary Nordlie's one-two punch for shallow-water bass. He fishes them on the same rig he uses for all his smallmouth fishing, a lightweight Fenwick 6½-foot, graphite spinning rod and a spinning reel loaded with 6-pound-test line.

"Smallies can be fussy when it comes to the action they want," says Nordlie. "One day, they want the lure brought back on a steady retrieve. The next day, you can let the lure lay where it lands until the rings have all disappeared and then give it a little twitch. I've given up trying to outguess them; I just let them make the decision for me, and then I give them what they want."

Surface plugs work best when the water is calm. If the water is rippled or the surface plugs don't entice the fish, Nordlie switches to live bait.

"Sure, you can catch smallmouth bass on crankbaits and spinnerbaits when they won't hit on the surface," he says, "but I've found that nothing beats live bait when the fish are feeding below the surface. Beside, those lures are expensive, and the rocks will just eat 'em up. When I snag up using live bait, all I'm going to lose is a hook and sinker or maybe a jighead. Knowing that, I'm more likely to go ahead and toss my bait into places where a snag is likely. More often than not, those are the same places the fish hang out."

Two techniques work best for Nordlie. He fishes a 3-inch Mister Twister tail on a ¹/₁₆-ounce jighead and tips it with leech or piece of crawler. It takes some time to develop the touch you need to keep the jig swimming just over the rocks. Most anglers get discouraged after hanging up several times and quit. But if you stay with it, you will develop the "touch," and then you have the most dependable fish-catching technique always at your disposal. Nothing beats a jig. Even when fished without bait, a jig resembles everything a smallie feeds on naturally. Learn to fish a jig, and you can nearly always catch smallies.

The second technique is slip-bobber fishing. A lot of Nordlie's customers are not avid anglers, they really are not interested in learning to fish a jig. All they want to do is have a good time and catch a bunch of fish without the hassle of being snagged all the time. The slip bobber is the answer. Adjust the bobber stop so the bait (usually a leech) dangles about a foot above bottom. A hook, split-shot, bobber and slip-knot—what could be easier?

## Shallow-Water Fishing

If you fish in shallow water or on the shore, search for any submerged branches or trees along it. Use worms, crickets, shrimp and other live or once live baits either with bobbers (to prevent nasty tangles) or without. You can catch any number of bass, catfish, crappie, or perch, as well as (if up north) pike and muskellunge.

*Tracy Benton*
*Boca Raton, FL*

## Sharp Hook Test

One way to test the sharpness of a hook is to balance it on your fingernail—if it skids off, it's not sharp enough. It should stay on the nail. Good test for crankbait hooks. Sharp hooks mean more fish.

*Jeff Swarthout*
*Barryton, MI*

## A Photo is Worth a Thousand Words

**K**eep a disposable camera (in a waterproof bag) in your boat at all times in case you forget to bring your camera. A trophy fish without a camera can quickly become a fish tale.

*Joe Johnson*
*Apple Valley, MN*

## Get the Kinks Out

**T**o get rid of the kinks and twists in your fishing line, remove your lure, swivel, etc. and let your bare line out into the water (as far as you need to) as you motor across: or let the current carry and straighten it. Then reel in.

*Joe Johnson*
*Apple Valley, MN*

## Staying Warm While Cold-Weather Fishing

**T**his tip is for the angler who loves cold weather fishing, but gets too chilled to stay on the water. Take a t-shirt and sew pockets from any material (other old shirts work great) onto it. I scatter them on the chest, stomach and back. When you go out in the cold, place handwarmers in the pockets and you'll stay warm a lot longer.

*Steffan Howell*
*Princeton, WV*

## Tips for Taking Iced-Over Fish

**I**t's not a bad idea to begin fishing with a vibrating "search" lure, to at least "call" fish into your ice-fishing hole. Examples include the Cicada, Sonar, Knocker Minnow and the Rattl'n Rapala.

If you get a lot of "follows" with these lures, try tipping them with maggots or even fish eyes (where legal) for more strike-triggering appeal.

Also, learn to "call" fish into your hole with a search lure, reel it up, and quickly drop a smaller, more subtle bait. That often results in an immediate bite.

Be constantly alert for suspended fish to pass into your sonar signal. Quickly reel up or let down to them.

Don't stay more than 10 or 15 minutes in one hole without a bite, unless you're on a known hotspot and believe strongly fish will move to you soon. However, if you've just driven up in your pickup and punched a hole with a power auger, you'll need to let the fish "settle down." Some anglers pre-drill holes and come back later to fish them. Also, if you catch a few quick fish in a hole and the bite slows—even if you still see fish on the sonar screen—move to a new hole. One of the only drawbacks to using sonar through the ice is that people get addicted to the "video game" of trying to make fish bite.

Realize that, while fish often bite readily during the prime hours of dusk and dawn, they can often be caught all day with the right approach. At midday, fish are not normally willing to move far to bite, so you have to put the bait right in front of them and tease them into striking. Live bait, and beyond that fresh live bait, is crucial. Don't try to see how many fish you can catch on the same maggot, or minnow.

# Taking Sunfish in Deep Water

Taking big sunfish consistently from shallow-water haunts is easy. But when extremes of summer heat or winter cold drive them down into deeper water, catching them can be difficult and requires special fishing techniques.

To master deep-water fishing, you should first understand why fish move to deep water. To do that, think of a lake or pond as a triple-decker sandwich cookie—two thick layers of cookie with a thinner layer of cream filling between them. In summer, many lakes and ponds stratify into three layers, with the warmest, oxygen-rich water on top, cold oxygen-free water on bottom, and a middle layer of cool, oxygen-rich water called the thermocline in between. The thermocline, like the filling in the cookie, is the best part, because that's where deep-water sunfish are likely to concentrate. Of the three layers, this one usually best satisfies the sunfish's needs for dissolved oxygen and water temperature.

The depth and thickness of the thermocline will vary from one body of water to another. In some ponds, it may be 5 feet down and only a foot thick; in extremely large, deep lakes, it may go 20 feet down and several feet thick. Regardless of its location and size, though, the thermocline is where nearly all sizable sunfish will be during periods of temperature extremes. And though the thermocline doesn't occupy the deepest part of the lake or pond, it's still far deeper than the thin layer of surface water most sunfish anglers usually fish.

To locate deep-water sunfish, first locate the thermocline. This is relatively simple. Lower a thermometer into the water and take temperature readings at various depths. The temperature will probably change very little the first several feet, but at some point—usually between 5 to 20 feet deep—the temperature will drop quickly, falling 5 to 10 degrees within a fairly short distance. Viola! You have found the thermocline, and this is the depth you should fish.

Okay, so now you've identified the band of water where deepwater sunfish are likely to be. What next? A depth sounder will help you locate cover or structure where sunfish might concentrate—a channel dropoff, and underwater hump, the edge of an inundated pond or perhaps a cluster of tall stumps beneath the surface. If you don't have a depth sounder, look for topside features that appear to continue underwater to the desired depth—bridge or dock pilings, long steeply sloping points, rocky ledges, toppled trees or the outside edge of a weedbed.

Once you've found such areas, you're ready to fish. And when fishing deep water, nothing can beat an ultra-light rod and a tiny reel filled with 2- or 4-pound test line. This rig exhibits sensitivity not found with larger tackle and permits you to detect the most delicate nibbles. It also turns every fish you hook, into a whopper. Fighting a ¾-pound bluegill up out of 15 feet of water on 2-pound line and a mere switch of a rod isn't as easy as it sounds.

A tightline live bait set-up is the best choice for taking bottom-feeding sunfish in areas where the thermocline touches the lake bed. Thread a slip sinker on your line, and, below it, tie on a barrel swivel just large enough to keep the sinker from sliding off. To the swivel's lower eye, tie a 2- or 3-foot leader of light line tipped with a small, light-wire hook. Add your favorite live bait—worms, crickets and larvae baits are excellent choices—then cast the rig out, and allow it to settle to the bottom. When a sunfish takes the bait, the line moves freely through the sinker with no resistance to alert fish to a possible threat.

If fish seem persnickety, do away with the sinker altogether. Without any weight except that of the hook, a cricket or worm sinks very, very slowly, providing almost irresistible allure to down-under sunnies. As the bait sinks, watch the line very closely for any slight movement indicating a hit.

Fly rod anglers can also score heavily on deep-water sunfish. Wet flies resembling insect larvae and nymphs are especially effective. A sinking fly line can carry these patterns down where big sunfish are feeding and produce pleasing results. Work the flies in short hops. The sight of such a fidgety tidbit is certain to tempt even the most jaded piscatorial taste buds.

If sunfish are suspended, try fishing a small jig under a bobber. If they aren't deeper than the length of your rod or pole, you can merely clamp a plastic bobber on your line, and dangle the jig below it at the proper depth. When you cast, the jig sinks to the right depth and stays there while you retrieve it with twitches that lend a lifelike action.

If sunfish are deeper than your rod is long, rig a sliding bobber above the jig to make casting easier. To do this, tie a short piece of rubber band around your line at the depth you want to fish. When the bobber hits the water, the weight of the jig pulls line through the bobber until the rubber band abuts the float. Your jig is automatically at the depth you selected, and you can easily adjust the depth by moving the rubber up or down the line. The knot will easily pass through your line guides and wind onto the reel spool. It's simple and effective.

If you're tired of catching scrawny little sunfish, search out the depths during summer and winter. That's where the big ones will usually be. Deep-water fishing fills what might otherwise be an empty spot on your fishing itinerary, and that's worth fishing in the heat and the cold.

# Patience and Persistence Pay Off

I decided to go fishing in a nearby pond one day. I started out with my fly rod and small poppers but had no success, so I switched to a light spinning outfit and started catching very aggressive, hard-hitting peacock bass. Shaped like a large bluegill, they have a bright orange/red breast and a dark spot on their rounded tail. I hooked and released about twenty of them, but kept one for a picture.

Because I had a couple of very hard hits and I saw a swirl from what I thought was a bass chasing my small crankbait, I tied on a larger bait and after a couple of casts, was astonished to have a snook hit the lure, make a complete sommersault out of the water and then break off, apparently cutting the light line on his gill cover.

I tied on a second lure with the same results. Another good hit, another lure lost. So I ended that outing and returned the next morning with a heavier rod and line. After two or three casts, I hooked and landed a 30-inch snook (8 pounds). About a week later, I landed another snook—33-inches (13 pounds)—but I released that one. Then, as the weather and water temperatures warmed, things quieted down. So I changed my tactics and switched to a soft plastic bait, rigged with a slip sinker. I would cast, count down about 6 or 8 seconds, and after a few tries, again hooked a 32-inch snook—which I released.

My tip is: Be patient and persistent. If what worked once doesn't work again—try something different.

*Carl E. Zahrte*
*Parma, OH*

# Care and Feeding Minnows

Anyone who has ever kept fish knows that bait is difficult to preserve. Savvy bait dealers keep minnows and baitfish in cool, aerated water. Ideally, baitfish should be lively and bright-looking. They should not have damaged skin, red noses from bumping into tanks or missing scales from too much handling. Good bait "balls up" in a tank corner near the bottom; bad bait skitters about near the surface or just bellies-up. Good bait wiggles wildly while being transferred from tank to net; bad bait just flops. Don't pay for hardy baitfish and then take a fragile substitute! Insist on an oxygenated bag, if available.

Most fishermen who complain about poor quality of today's minnows create more problems with poor care, over-crowded containers, high temperatures or lack of oxygen.

Minnows do best if they're not crowded. Figuring on a fish-per-gallon basis, 18 small minnows or six large ones are the limit. Separate cylindrical gallon containers work well for small batches of minnows. This encourages you to try more than one type, and cylindrical containers help head off "corner pileup" and the resulting injuries that damage minnows in rectangular tanks. Old water jugs also make excellent minnow buckets.

Place the bait buckets in a large container, such as a big cooler. The cooler keeps the buckets from rolling about or upsetting. Add some ice and it will keep your minnow bucket's water temperature between 50 and 65 degrees. Remove any dead or dying minnows and save them in a sealable plastic bag on ice for use as cut bait or chum. An alternative would be to place bags of ice or, even better, frozen cartons of water in your minnow container to keep things cool.

Oxygen is also a necessary ingredient. Some bait shops offer bait bagged in water from their own oxygenated tank. The sealed bag is then placed in a box and, if kept cool, should keep minnows in good shape for a couple of days. (This is, after all, the way tropical fish are shipped from Brazil to Florida and other U.S. destinations.) As water temperature rises, water loses its ability to hold oxygen and crowding becomes a critical factor. Battery-powered aerators work off car, boat or flashlight batteries; 110-volt aquarium aerators will handle large bait-stock tanks at home. Stop-gap methods include using oxygen tablets that create bubbles, stirring water with an egg beater or removing water and shaking it up in a barrel. And then there is the method applied by a Kansas teenager: a funnel and rubber hose. Clamped to the car windows, the funnel faces forward with the hose leading to the bait container. The faster the teenager drove, the more oxygen bubbles there were in the water.

Trolling buckets and other drag-along containers work very well for boaters when surface waters are cool; however, they are poor choices when surface temperatures rise in summer. These buckets can't be left in the water when the boat is traveling at high speeds, either. Shore anglers who put their minnow buckets in a lake or stream find that their minnows turn fins-up. They should move them to a spot where current, or wave action, will help ensure more adequate oxygenation. Sinking a minnow bucket to deeper, cooler water can improve survival rates, too.

Live shiners can take gamefish when all else fails. However, keeping shiners and other delicate species from doing the backstroke without an aerator can be a problem. Aerators do quit for one reason or another. It's best to have a backup or alternative system if the aerator fails.

# Stay on Those Fish

When fishing big water, finding the fish and staying with them can be hard. Once you find them, mark them with a buoy. The one thing a buoy does is they show you which way you're drifting. Even with all new electronics, it is hard to get back to the spot as fast. And you can judge how to make the next drift. In the ocean where I fish most of the time, the drift can change real fast. This makes it easier to find the fish since they will try to stay behind the structure most of the time. Even GPS takes you longer to figure which way you will drift by watching the buoy, it makes it easy. Then remember to keep the lines straight down—don't let them string out. You might have to back into it with the motor to keep them straight down. It is better than adding more weight or tying lost gear.

*E. Scott Dilley*
*Yakima, WA*

# Cast at Jumping Minnows

When you see minnows jumping out of the water, cast a floating Rapala out in the middle of it then run it slow, then begin picking up speed.

*Jeff Swarthout*
*Barryton, MI*

# Looking for White Bass

I recently started gaining an interest in white bass fishing, what with good white bass waters like the St. Croix and Mississippi Rivers near my home. The old adage is, look for swirling gulls and you will find the white bass below them, churning up the water.

But the first time I ever saw white bass working the surface, I didn't know what I was seeing. In the first place, there weren't any gulls flocking overhead. In the second place, the water wasn't being churned to a froth. There were some swirls, and fins and tails bulging out of the water, but had I not been with someone who had seen this before, I would have written it off as carp tailing on the surface.

The lessons here are several. One, the gulls can help you find white bass, but the birds aren't always available. Two, if you're not seeing gulls, look for the gentle, rolling-swirling-smacking surface disturbance described. Three, try to fish on a calm day when this relatively gentle surface activity will be easily visible. Four, don't forget your binoculars because they will come in handy.

As for fishing, don't go barging through a school of white bass once you find it. Use an electric trolling motor or oars to hold yourself 20 yards or so off the edge of the activity. Cast across the activity and reel into it. When you catch a fish, unhook it and get back to fishing as soon as possible — there will be time later to put them in the cooler or live well. And stay mobile — the school might go down for a minute and then surface 20 yards away. It's fun!

*Tom Carpenter*
*Plymouth, MN*

## Locating Ice-Time Sunfish

In many lakes, sunfish are the most common ice-fishing catch, and right after ice-up is a top time to catch them. Places you caught sunfish in summertime are often good early-winter locations. In fact, before the ice forms is a great time to find areas. You'll find bluegills elsewhere, but the best places are weedy points, bars and, especially, bays of just several feet deep or less. Big bluegills commonly lurk near the bases of the thick weeds, or if available, rocks, stumps and brush. Often overlooked in winter are small farm ponds. Again check for sunfish-holding cover, possibly near the pond's dam.

On a lake you've never fished, a bait shop operator may be able to tell you the whereabouts of the bays and points. (Or if it's big bull bluegills you're after, the operator might be able to recommend a special lake.) If available, a lake map, of course, also helps locate top general structure, and once the ice forms, you can use a handline or, quicker yet, sonar to find the right depths. You can look for weeds or wood through the ice hole in clear water, or use sonar or a handline.

Some years, early-ice sunfishing starts before Halloween in the most-northerly reaches. For most anglers, though, it's around December or later. The main consideration is safe ice thickness: clear lake ice at least 2 inches thick is necessary to support the weight of one person; at least 3 inches for a few people widely separated, and about one foot for a car or light pickup. (Double these figures for slushy ice or weak dark ice. Also, river ice is generally weaker than lake ice.)

There's one exception to the safe-ice rule. An interesting brand of ice fishing can be enjoyed where docks or piers remain on the lake through the winter. Even if the ice is only an inch thick, you can walk out on the dock or pier (as long as it's not slippery) and break holes in the ice at various depths with a chisel or ax. The longer docks or piers offer a good selection of water depths as well as cover preferred by sunfish.

## Pining for Panfish

Here are a few observations on panfish. I've fished for panfish all of my life and have found that almost all of their forage is 15 feet or less from shore. So to catch panfish, you sure don't need to have a boat. Also, I tend to fish ponds (especially farm ponds) for panfish. These waters don't have much fishing pressure so the fish are usually bigger. I've caught crappie weighing from 1- to 2 1/2-pounds and redear (sunfish) nearly that big. I hope this information helps other panfish fanatics.

*Aarron Johnson*
*Fountain City, IN*

## Think Small for Panfish

You will catch a lot more panfish if you use a dime-size bobber and the smallest hook you can get away with. The fish won't feel any pull on that small bobber and you will have him!

*Bill Stalego*
*Newark, OH*

# Use Rubber Bands as Bobber Stops

I cut my own rubber bands from the fingers of latex surgical gloves and use them for bobber stops when ice fishing instead of store bought rubber bands. They are limber and go through the rod guides a lot better without hanging up.

*Peter Honnick*
*Constantia, NY*

# Make Your Own Sand Seat

If you would like to give your legs a break while surf or bank fishing, try my lightweight "sand seat." It consists of a $1/2$-inch plywood seat resting on a flange atop a 48-inch, $1^1/4$-inch diameter of wooden dowel (pointed on the bottom). About 30 inches below the seat, another piece of plywood, flange and stop tube prevent the dowel from sinking too far into the sand. Trim the bottom of the dowel so you can stand with your legs straight and lean back on the seat in comfort.

*Ronald Inch*
*Etobicoke, Ontario, Canada*

# Easy Detangling

Often times when fishing spinnerbaits, spinning rigs or even adding line to your spool, your line will twist creating annoying tangles and causing lost fishing time. To eliminate twisted line, remove your bait and tackle from the line and let out at least twice the amount of line you anticipate fishing with while boating to your next location. Allow a few minutes for the line to untwist. By the time you get to the next fishing hole, your line should be ready to go.

*Terry Brodsky*
*Minnetonka, MN*

# The Homer Rhode Loop Knot

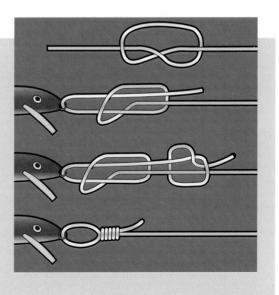

Here is a knot that I find to be strong and easy to tie. The Homer Rhode Loop Knot. Here's how: Tie a simple overhand knot about four inches from the end of the line. Pass the end of the line through the lure eye, then back through the center of the overhand knot. With the end of the line, make another overhand knot around the standing part of the line. When tightened, the two overhand knots jam together, forming a loop. Where the second overhand knot is positioned determines the size of the loop. For a big loop, form the second overhand knot well up the standing line; for a small one, make it close to the first knot.

*Lester McConnell*
*Los Alamos, NM*

# Night Fishing with Cyalume Lightsticks

**S**cotch tape or twist tie cyalume to your rod tip when night fishing.

Add cyalume lightstick to inline planer board when trolling for walleye at night. Drill a small hole in the top side of the planer board.

*Matthew Radzialowski*
*Wixom, MI*

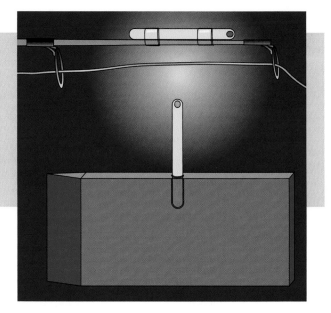

# Preserve the Environment

**A** friend and I were fishing at Lake Casitas, California, when we spotted a Western grebe with fishing line tightly wrapped around its neck, wing and left foot. The poor thing could scarcely move, let alone navigate. We caught the bird and cut the line off before letting it go free. Throwing old fishing line in the water is stupid. Discarded line endangers wildlife and fouls motors. Please think twice before discarding fishing line.

*Michael Buck*
*Carpinteria, CA*

# A Better Ice Cube

**B**efore I go on long fishing or camping trips, I save small plastic water bottles. I then fill these 12- to 16-ounce bottles with tap water and freeze them. I take the frozen bottles and line my cooler with them. They melt slower than ice cubes and the water stays contained in the bottles. No more soggy mess. And, not only that, the melt-water also becomes my emergency water supply, should I need it.

*Kong Shang*
*Reno, NV*

# The Bass Spawn

Pre-spawn behavior and spawning movements to the shallows are dictated by the length of day, the amount of sunlight and the water temperature. The angle of the sun and the sequence of moon cycles are also involved in pre-spawning behavior. This phase is usually in the spring between the months of February and June when the days lengthen.

When the water temperature reaches somewhere between 58 and 62 degrees, most largemouth are in a pre-spawn phase. When the temperature reaches the mid 60s, the majority of females will be hovering over a bed. However, some bass have been found to actually go on the bed in water temperatures as low as 50 degrees. Others have successfully spawned in 75-degree water. The fact remains that the process of spawning takes longer when water temperatures are colder.

Unusually frigid spring weather followed by an abrupt change to unseasonably hot weather can quickly cause elevated water temperatures. Then a female's egg mass may ripen rapidly and she may drop them all at once in just an hour or two "bedtime." Such hurried efforts are often in cold or uncleaned nests or in quickly prepared nests not suitable for a highly successful spawn.

Many researchers believe that the moon phase is related to the initiation of spawning activities. They say the amount of sunlight and sustained temperature are apparently right for the female to drop her eggs around a full moon. The majority of bass do seem to spawn then. Others may spawn on the dark of the moon. In rivers or tidal-influenced waters lunar effects may be negligible. In coastal estuaries the tides are minimal between the full- and new-moon periods. That's the ideal time for brackish-water bass to take on the job. Other environmental factors that affect tidewater fish are level fluctuations of a foot or more and the tide change two to four times each day.

Photoperiod (amount of sunlight) is generally thought to be the most important factor and the key to triggering the spawning process. Photoperiod alone does not determine spring bass locations, but surface temperature is probably more important at this time of year than at any other. Lakes typically have warm pockets of water that may vary 4 or 5 degrees over 300 yards. Such areas are the first to see actual spawning activity.

Weather influences on the spawning process are many. Slowly rising water temperatures are generally optimal for spawning success. Cold fronts drastically influence bass on a bed or disrupt the efforts of those moving in and out of the shallows trying to locate an affable partner and nest. They can also have an adverse effect on the success of the spawn.

Bass trying to move out of the pre-spawn phase to the beds will back away from the shallows to the more comfortable depths when a front arrives. With a slight drop in water temperature, they retreat to their deeper holding areas and may not move back for several days following a warming trend. If weather continues to interrupt the process and the spawn is not successful, the lake's partial or entire year-class can be effectively eliminated. Such results will upset the population balance of that fishery.

Water-level fluctuations can also have drastic effects on a successful spawn. Lakes with an erratic springtime water table have erratic bass production. Drawdowns for irrigation, flood control or other reasons adversely affect not only pre-spawn bass but also the spawning sites and the intended results of that activity. Disoriented bass and abandoned beds mean loss of eggs and a low production for that particular water.

Mature female bass that are not able to spawn are often in a predicament. Some bass in the pre-spawn stage actually skip the spawn and go directly into the post-spawn period. Their egg mass is simply absorbed by the body. Others may develop "roe rot." This means the egg mass hardens during the female's unsuccessful attempt to spawn and the bass eventually dies.

# A Catch-and-Release Strategy and Philosophy

We live and fish in a great day and age, with a catch-and-release ethic that is alive and well. Here is one strategy and philosophy I have come to believe in, when it comes to releasing a fish unharmed:

If a hook is buried deep (beyond the fish's jaws or mouth), clip your line or leader, leave the hook in and let the fish go. Its metabolism will make short order of the metal hook, and the fish has an exponentially bigger chance of living because his gullet and innards will not have been ripped and ruptured as you pull and dig the hook out.

That's the strategy part. The philosophy is this: Sure, it might take a little time to re-rig, but it will take a lot longer for the waters to grow that fish again. And the little investment of minutes and money it takes is a small price to pay to know that the fish is out there, healthy, and going to be available to be caught again—maybe by me—someday.

This plan only presents a problem when you're using highly expensive lures. Then, a good tactic is to clip the deep trebles with a wire cutter, leaving the "bad" ones embedded in the fish. Carry extra trebles in your tackle box, to replace the ones you might lose. When live bait fishing for pike, I have also been known to "unclip" the hook when it's in a pike's throat, leaving the hook in the fish but my wire leader intact. Then all I have to do is snap on a new hook!

*Tom Carpenter*
*Plymouth, MN*

# Do-It-Yourself Hook Disgorger

After tiring of tearing up my fly heads with a needle-nose pliers, I devised a handy, do-it-yourself hook disgorger. All you need is a stick from an ice cream treat and a sharp pocket knife. Narrow one end of the stick so it will easily fit inside the mouth of a panfish or trout. Cut a notch in the narrow end and you're done. The disgorger works great with flies, bait hooks and jigs—and best of all, the price is right.

*Gerald Coates*
*Parks, NE*

# Add Resilience to Old, Brittle Fishing Line

If you have monofilament line in your garage and it has become brittle, just soak the whole spool in a bucket of water for a couple of hours. It replaces the water content in the line and makes it easier to handle. Monofilament line is 9 percent water. I heard this at a seminar from a company representative. It works.

*Kevin P. Studley*
*Port Richey, FL*

# Walleyes in the Wood

On many bodies of water, typically rivers and reservoirs, weed growth is limited or even nonexistent. Here, brush and timber may be the only shallow-water cover available, but they offer a food source and shade the same as weeds do.

This type of cover includes submerged stump fields, beaver lodges, flooded timber or brush, fallen trees and even sunken logs. Prime locations are those near deep water. A timbered flat or point near a ledge or creek channel, for example, is much better than one with no deep areas nearby. A tree toppled onto a shallow flat is less likely to hold walleyes than a tree which has fallen into deep water from a steep bank.

Timber will hold walleyes from spring through fall. However, the fish use flooded brush mainly in the spring as water levels rise. Timber may even hold sauger (shown at right) at times, especially in spring, but the saugers will be down deeper than the walleyes.

They will stay in the brush as long as the water rises or remains stable. But to avoid becoming landlocked, they quickly move deeper the moment levels begin to drop.

Just like weeds, the edges of timber are prime locations to fish. More aggressive, but smaller, walleyes will be located there. But don't be afraid to explore the denser cover where larger fish tend to hide.

# Non-Slip Filleting Board

Filleting fish can be a slippery process. Many manufacturers have come out with modern fillet boards that cost a lot of money. My favorite surface is the Sunday newspaper. Take several layers of unfolded newspaper and place them on your fillet table. Place the fish on the newspaper and fillet both sides. Notice how the fish does not slip, allowing you to work quickly and more safely. When both sides of the fish are done, wrap the remains in one or two layers of the newpaper and discard. Not only have you made filleting easier, but you found another use for old newspaper.

*Terry Brodsky*
*Minnetonka, MN*

# Floating Net

Ever drop a landing net, gaff or boat hook over the gunwale? Good-bye! Here's how to keep them afloat next time that happens. Just remove the plastic cap on the end of the handle and fill the hollow interior with foam packing or expandable foam. No more worry because now it floats!

*Stanley Buchacz*
*LaGrange Park, IL*

# Waterproof Your Boots

My tip is for the member who loves to fish in cold, wet weather, but doesn't have waterproof boots. Take four plastic grocery bags and put two around the outside of each boot liner. Put your foot inside the liner and pull the boot on over the bags. If the tops of the bags stick out, tuck them in and no one will know the difference. Meanwhile, your feet will stay warm and dry—even if your boots leak.

*Jon Werner*
*Grove City, MN*

# Swallowed Hook Remedy

Bullheads and catfish often swallow the hook when they take a bait. Many anglers I know simply cut the line and retrieve the hook later, when they clean the fish. I have found a better way—one that allows me to release the fish unharmed. Just swap your regular bait hook for a jig, then tip it with your favorite bait and fish it like you would otherwise. The cats and bullheads will still bite, but they will rarely swallow the whole rig.

*Richard Nusser*
*Morton Grove, IL*

# Work Your Bobber

Why is it that some fisherman throw out a bobber and expect the fish to do the rest? For me, bobber fishing is not about taking the easy way out. I have a different method that I prefer. Rather than using a drab old plastic bobber, I put on a balsa pencil float and a jig. After the float and jig hit the water, I wait a few seconds and then start twitching my wrist downward. The fish love it.

*Brian Ahern*
*Berwyn, IL*

## Post-Spawn Crappies

Post-spawn crappies in all waters gradually move into the deeper summer haunts. Search the deep water nearest the spawning sites, near forage involving easy-to-catch prey, ranging from tiny fish to small crayfish to insects.

While recuperating from spawning, the fish aren't always easy to capture. On natural lakes, slow-troll or drift jigs or lip-hooked minnows as you search with your sonar unit for suspended crappies at lake ends, bay centers or near down-lake points.

Post-spawners in clear mountain lakes may suspend 15 feet or deeper in cove middles, points and near main-lake woody bluffs. Crappies in dingy lakes, though, may remain more object-oriented in their post-spawn activities.

During post-spawn in rivers, the water usually lowers at the oxbows and sloughs. Using sonar and trolling the 10- to 15- foot-deep centers is best unless it's murky, and fish are swimming shallower in available woody cover.

# Sentimental Slip Bobber

Make a sentimental slip bobber. Take the cork from a bottle of wine after being used to celebrate something. Saw it in half (two little ones are better than one big one) and drill a hole through the cork pieces end-wise, if the corkscrew hasn't done it for you. Force a coffee stirrer through each cork piece. Paint if you desire.

*Richard Richter*
*Michigan City, IN*

## Electric Trolling Motor Handle

I discovered an easy to install, inexpensive extension handle for electric trolling motors. A plastic golf club tube will fit snugly over most tiller handles. Even if you have to do a little adjusting or tapping to get a tight fit, it's still cheaper than buying an extension!

*Paul Skredsvig*
*Stanwood, WA*

## Locating Ice-Time Crappies

In some regions, the most sought-after ice species is the crappie, which readily hits ice fishermen's offerings. Generally, look for winter crappies to suspend near structure or cover, but their depth may vary widely. In frozen Mississippi River backwaters, crappies may swim in only two feet of water, while in a deep natural lake, crappies are commonly caught at 20 to 30 feet. However, as a general rule, many early winter crappies hover in rather shallow water, and they're near cover such as weedlines, weedy flats, brush, stumps, sunken boats and rock piles. In early winter, the bottom and mid-depths often lure crappies.

Additionally, enclosed heated crappie fishing docks are common on some southern and Midwestern reservoirs. They're excellent fishing sites during unsafe early (or late) ice. For a small fee, you're in business; you can usually quickly find crappies around the docks' cover which is usually brush piles. Also, fisherman here who are experienced in fishing the dock may share fish catching information with first-timers.

## Help with Hook Sharpening

I found it nearly impossible to hold a hook for sharpening. To solve the problem, I cut a small block of wood, sawed a channel down its length at a varied depth, and drilled hook "eye holes" at intervals. This "vise" holds hooks of all sizes steady as a rock while protecting the line and knot from damage. I pass a stone, at a controlled angle, down both sides of the point and it is sharp!

*Robert L. Josephs*
*Palm Bay, FL*

## No-Slip Knots

A good tip that I would recommend is to use glue on your knots. Instead of using the expensive fishing glue, just use a super adhesive glue. I haven't had a knot slip since I started using this method. I used to have knots slip all the time on superlines.

*Scott Murphy*
*Lacey, WA*

## Don't Let Slip Floats Slip Off

Slip floats are great tools for many situations, except when a snag or a big fish parts your line. Unless there's something left to stop it, the float will slide off the end of the line and you'll either have to chase it or lose it. Instead, put a second float stop (or stop knot) about 12 inches above the terminal tackle—the place where most breaks occur. It will prevent the float from slip-sliding away.

*Dick Craig*
*Eden Prairie, MN*

## Finding the Right Flats

"If you aren't familiar with the water," says Larry Williams, Largemouth bass expert, "look at a good map and circle those areas where the contour lines are far apart. Ideally, the flat will be about 5 feet deep, but it can be as much as 15 feet, depending on water clarity. It will be on or near a north shore and have deep water nearby. In a man-made impoundment, that deep water is usually a submerged creek or river channel."

Williams explains that it's a bonus to have some kind of cover on the flat, even if it's only scattered. Weeds or brush piles will better attract and hold both prey and predator. Still, cover is more relative than mandatory. If a lake has little or none, a bare flat may do just fine.

The slope of the flat is also relative. Williams prefers one that doesn't drop more than a few feet in a hundred yards. But again, it all depends on what the rest of the lake has to offer. As for size, he says a 30- to 40-acre flat is ideal, five acres is too small, and no flat can be too large.

## Thunderstorm Fishing

I go trout fishing right before a thunderstorm. The fish go feeding at this time. Worms are best after the storm.

*Jeff Swarthout*
*Barryton, MI*

## Bass Tactic

Faced with a deep, clear lake? Is the sun high in the sky? Is the boat traffic heavy? Time to fish deep or go home. Look for mudlines next to shore and fish a finesse bait in the mudline. Remember, this lake is the fish's home. It has to adapt to survive and some fish will utilize the mudline. Everybody else is fishing deep ... these fish don't get pressured. Also a good place to twitch a small balsa minnow bait. Fish quietly!

*Homer Lee*
*East Stroudsburg, PA*

## Fishing Carrier

This is a carrier I made out of 1-inch x 6-inch pine for the frame with ¼-inch plywood sides and ½-inch foam inserts. The length of the box is determined by the trolling motor shaft. Included in the box is a portable transducer bracket, along with fish-on rod holders, a spare prop and a jumper cable for portable sonar.

*Bob Kjos*
*Republic, WA*

## Ice Cube Alternative

One of the best ways to keep your catch fresh is to use a five gallon bucket with a lid. Put water in the bucket and cover it with the lid so the fish won't splash it out. Also, take a ¹/₂ gallon plastic milk jug or a 2 liter soda bottle, fill it about ²/₃ full with water and freeze it. After it freezes, put the bottle in the bucket and take it fishing. It will keep your catch fresh and cool the whole day. The bucket also makes a nice little table or seat.

*James Pratt*
*Clayton, IL*

## Clean Your Fishing Equipment

I fish 90 percent saltwater. After a day on the water, I wash down all of my equipment and tackle with a few drops of dish detergent. After everything is dry, I spray the rods and reels completely inside and out with automotive silicone spray, but make sure the can doesn't say "Do not use on rubber or plastic". Make sure you spray inside the guides. You can feel the difference when you are casting. I also spray all of my metal spoons.

*Kevin P. Studley*
*Port Richey, FL*

## Stay-Put Tackle Box

I was fishing with two friends of mine and my tackle box slid off the aluminum seat and landed upside down. That is when I got this idea! I took an old, rubber floor mat that was in my garage and glued it to the bottom of my tackle box. It also does a good job of staying put in the back bed of my pick up truck.

*William Lefever*
*Massillon, OH*

## Finding Your Hotspot Again

No problem finding your lake hotspot when returning to fish again. Just use my fail-safe method of location without using a GPS. All you have to do is jot down locations on shore that line up with where you are catching fish and when you return, there won't be a ton of boats on the spot because you used a marker. Be sure to pick out immovable objects on shore. If you must use a marker, don't put it on the spot but off to the side and remember where it's at when you anchor. I like to be at least a cast away.

*Stephen Turnis*
*Dubuque, IA*

## Getting Bluegills in a Feeding Mood

As an old saying goes, bluegills are where you find them. But there are times when you've found them that they stop feeding after a couple are caught, as if the head bluegill says: "Okay, guys and gals, at ease!" Mick Thill, fishing ace, has a clever tactic for such times.

He carries a magnum slingshot with rubber bands to propel a pouchful of grubs up to about 50 feet. He fires a volley, then waits to see if feeding action results. If not, he lays a pouchful in another direction. Once he triggers even one bluegill to begin eating these decoy maggots, others are sure to follow.

Although he prefers to fish from shore where most match fishing is done, he is just as adept moving about in a boat, seeking bluegill hangouts wherever they might be. He showed me a clipping in his scrapbook, written by Bob Bledsoe, outdoor editor of the Tulsa Tribune.

They set out on a frigid November day on the Illinois River when even the veterans were getting zilched. Thill uncorked his super-ultra-light bag of grub tricks to come through with nine species of fish! Bledsoe's column gave a glowing appraisal of Thill's skills.

# Fish the Seams for Stream Trout

There are many places for trout to hold in a stream — a deep hole, below a log jam, behind a boulder, beneath an undercut bank ... the list goes on. These are obvious places that most everyone knows to look for, and fishes hard. So what do you do when you try all these trouty-looking spots but nothing produces?

Try "seams" where currents of different speeds, or directions, meet. Not only do these places collect food, but they also offer a spot for trout to "hold" and rest in the current as they wait for food to come drifting in. If these spots are in a bend in the stream, all the better.

Seams are not hard to spot. Wear polarized sunglasses (even on a cloudy day) to cut glare, and watch for the "lines" that indicate places where currents of different speeds or directions come together.

If you're live bait fisherman, flip your bait lightly upstream of the seam, and let your offering drift into the area naturally with the current. Use as little split shot as possible to get your bait down. If you're spin-fishing with a spinner or other lure, cast upstream and bounce the bait along the with the

current, to act like an injured minnow; give the bait extra "pause" in and around the seam, controlling it with a short line and thinking: "I want that lure to look like a crippled minnow or crayfish." If you're fly fishing, you're on your own, because I'm not a fly fisherman; but I would guess a streamer worked through the area, down along bottom where the trout will be holding, would do the job.

*Tom Carpenter*
*Plymouth, MN*

# Catching Pre-Spawn Crappies

As the days lengthen and water warms into the 50s and low 60s, lake crappies move toward spawning grounds. Pre-spawn fish often hold near cover at drop-offs slightly deeper than the spawning sites. (The fish often spawn around the depth at which a water clarity disk disappears, although thick reeds can provide the cover for them to spawn shallower. To check clarity, you can use anything white and roughly plate-sized, such as an anchor painted white.) On warm days, look for cover in backwater areas, open water areas nearby, and inlets and outlets. If you can't see cover, clues to fish location include insects-commonly eaten at this time—and minnows near the surface.

Pre-spawn reservoir fish, on warmer days, move shallower and shallower along a cove's old creek channel. Also check inlets, outlets and cover-laden flats adjacent to these channels. Around March in southern impoundments, fish may be 20 feet down in cool weather, but in 50-degree water on sunny afternoons, you might catch fish around cover that's just a few feet deep. In super-clear reservoirs on warmer days, try fishing at or near cover around backwater coves, main-lake areas, islands and along the edges of creek channels.

On rivers, check tailwater eddies, and look for spawning cover in backwater sloughs and connected lakes. "Papermouths" will lurk nearby, their depth being dependent upon the weather. In any water on cold days, crappies commonly suspend away from the warm-day sites.

# No-Rust Lids

I hate grabbing a jar of pork rind and finding the lid has rusted on. To remedy this, I cut a square piece of plastic wrap and place it between the "threads" on the glass jar and the metal lid.

*Rob Bippes*
*Mountain View, MO*

# Fishing Supplies

K eep a nail clipper, forceps and a small flashlight on a lanyard for easy access. This makes tying knots and extracting hooks very easy in day or night-time conditions.

*Dan Kennedy*
*Richfield, MN*

## Finding River Walleyes

P inpointing and ultimately catching river walleyes boils down to a simple two-part strategy. Recognizing the many slack-water areas in the current that attract baitfish is important in locating walleyes. Seldom will walleyes be found far from a readily available food source. Once these slack-water areas are identified, finding fish in them is simply a matter of checking as many likely spots as possible until fish are found.

Commonly referred to as current breaks, the slack-water areas of a river take on many forms. Anything jutting out into the flow of water, such as a point, fallen tree or wing dam, may represent a fishing hotspot. Water swirls around these obstructions and forms a slack-water area or eddy directly downstream. Also, a small slack-water area is formed along the front faces of wing dams, attracting walleyes during normal and low-water levels.

Obstruction on the bottom, such as rock piles, submerged stumps or logs, also form current breaks. Most submerged features can be located by watching for bubbles on the water's surface.

Still other current breaks that attract walleyes are natural depressions along the bottom and outside river bends that, through time, have been scoured out with deep holes.

Finally, wide stretches of river flats where there is slower current can also attract large numbers of walleyes. These flats can be especially good producers in the spring if they're dotted with patches of gravel, rock or rubble suitable for spawning.

Many angling methods can be utilized to catch walleyes holding in these slack-water areas. Vertical jigging and working the front face of wing dams are two of the most efficient and popular river-fishing strategies.

# Tubular Fish Basket

I like to fish crappie from a johnboat with no livewell, so keeping fish alive is a challenge. A 5-gallon bucket takes up a lot of room and gets in the way, so I use a floating fish basket. Some baskets that are designed to float will sink under the weight of a few fish. The solution is to put an 8-inch inner tube from a riding lawnmower around the neck of the basket, then inflate it. It fits nicely around the basket and will float a mess of fish.

*Kevin Firth*
*Woodward, OK*

# INDEX